THE LOUISVILLE ANTHOLOGY

THE LOUISVILLE ANTHOLOGY

EDITED BY **ERIN KEANE**

Belt Publishing

First Edition 2020
ISBN: 9781948742702

Belt Publishing
3143 W. 33rd Street, Cleveland, Ohio 44109
www.beltpublishing.com

Book design by Meredith Pangrace
Cover by David Wilson

CONTENTS

CONTENTS

Introduction:
A Letter from the Borderlands

ERIN KEANE

After living in Louisville for more than twenty-five years, I've learned that one of the fastest ways to start an argument here is to ask any group of people—locals, newcomers, curious bystanders alike—if this is the southernmost Midwestern city or the northernmost Southern town. Some declare with certainty that Kentucky's borders define it as Southern by default, while others argue that Louisville's position on the Ohio River gives the city more kinship with its neighbors to the north and west than with the commonwealth as a whole. This disagreement isn't likely to be resolved any time soon. Borderlands tend to defy easy characterizations. But the arguments on both sides reveal much about how Louisville straddles two worlds, and how the city does and does not reconcile its contradictions.

To be from this city is to be *from Louisville, not Kentucky*, I'm often told. As Dr. Lyman T. Johnson—a prominent twentieth-century Black educator whose discrimination lawsuit against the University of Kentucky resulted in the dismantling of a state law prohibiting integration of higher education institutions—famously said, "I break Kentucky into two parts, Louisville and the rest of the state. Louisville is oriented to the North, culturally and commercially. The rest of Kentucky looks to the South." In the twenty-first century, that difference in orientation also manifests itself politically, making *Louisville, not Kentucky* an electoral identity as well, the largest blue dot in a majority-red state.

Recently, I discovered a counterpoint to that view in this blunt assessment from *The Louisville Story*, a book by former school superintendent Omer Carmichael and journalist Weldon James about presiding over the desegregation of Louisville's public schools in the 1950s: "Louisville, like Kentucky, seceded after Appomattox."[1] Inside the tension of this contradiction, one can feel both the strain of Louisville pulling itself in the direction of progress and justice—often in the face of great opposition from within—and feel the sharp snap back when deep-rooted power, alarmed at the challenge, slams on the brakes.

1 | Adams, Luther. "Way Up North In Louisville: Migration and the Meaning of the South." In *Way Up North in Louisville: African American Migration in the Urban South*, 1930-1970, 37-58. University of North Carolina Press, 2010. Accessed March 3, 2020. doi:10.5149/9780807899434_adams.6.

Louisville, not Kentucky is a powerful story, and when conflicts arise with the rest of the state, some denizens of the city might even call for us to secede from the commonwealth. Ironic or not, there's always a hint of truth in these jokes. For the sake of argument, though, it's worth asking what kind of new, hypothetical independent civic entity, this *Louisville-Not-Kentucky*, would emerge from that exit. Would the city's deeply entrenched patterns of racial segregation and economic inequality remain? And if not, why do they persist now? In other words, if Louisville no longer existed in tension with or in a state of opposition to the rest of Kentucky, what new stories would the city be forced to tell about who or what it is and could be?

I am fascinated by the stories Louisville tells in part because I'm not from here. If I said this to a person hailing from anywhere else, they would be right to be confused. After all, I have taught classes and worked in offices and written books and danced to bands and fallen in and out of love here; learned how to drive, how to grow tomatoes, how to put two dollars across the board on the long shot, how to drink bourbon—and, crucially, how to know when to stop—all right here in this pocket of the Ohio River Valley, where a chenille blanket of pollen drifts over our heads a full ten months out of the year, for a quarter of a century now and counting, and surely that should make it official. And yet.

In shallow terms, I have neither high school allegiance nor home parish. My opinions on college basketball are weak. I lived here for at least eight years before I finally learned where "the old Sears building," a weirdly specific East End navigational lodestar, had once been. To this outsider at least, the Louisville some celebrate as being culturally superior to its surrounding environs—facing outward and upward, always moving in the direction of progress—seems at odds with the Louisville that is also caught, in many ways, in its own past. And yet, as one who was raised in a smaller conservative community across the state, I still choose Louisville for many reasons, some of which endure: Friday fish fries, rows of shotgun houses, the World Dainty Championship, the Portland and Central libraries, the Iroquois Amphitheatre, the cast iron façades of Museum Row. And some have now faded into memory: Jay's Cafeteria, Jake's Club Reno, the Dew Drop Inn. Indulge me on the now-defunct Louisville Falls Fountain, an enormous folly that shot 16,000 gallons of water per minute in a fleur-de-lis-shaped plume up, out of, and back into the Ohio River. Of course I'm not from here. How many locals over the years have chided my love of *that tacky old thing* and told me they were glad to see it scrapped? And yet I remember marveling at it on my first visit downtown, at its desire to impress—how I recognized that desire—and at its spectacular uselessness, so shameless in its artifice and flash. I confess I ache for it. Maybe it wasn't tasteful. If I alone choose it still, so be it.

Live in a city caught between *onward* and *remember-when* long enough, and you develop a personal palimpsest map almost in spite of yourself: Can we meet at the new place that used to be the other place that moved in after Flabby's, the Schnitzelburg bar with the legendary fried chicken, where the burn of an oyster shooter's hot sauce christened one of my most important apartment moves? A sign hanging outside a Newburg Road restaurant encourages passersby: *If you can't stop, please wave.* The Highlands eatery known by long-timers, despite all past or future names, as Kaelin's, has long claimed to be the birthplace of the cheeseburger, invented there in 1934 by founder Carl Kaelin. Periodically, the veracity of this claim comes under review, and the conclusion is usually a variation on, *So they say.* The truth of a place may be disputed or disrupted, the Kaelin's sign suggests, but its myths and legends can be acknowledged, even accepted on their own terms.

I may not be from Louisville, but I've spent a quarter of a century learning about it, and I have only scratched its surface. It started with a college friend pointing out how close we lived to "Daisy's house" from F. Scott Fitzgerald's *The Great Gatsby*, after an afternoon of coffee and browsing at the dearly departed Twice-Told Books on Bardstown Road. Daisy hailed from Louisville, where Jay Gatsby, a poor soldier, courted her during his brief stint at Louisville's Camp Taylor. Like Gatsby, Fitzgerald himself trained there during the first World War. In his novel, Fitzgerald describes Gatsby and Daisy sitting on her Louisville porch and taking romantic walks in a neighborhood that on the page sounds very much like the tony Cherokee Triangle, at the heart of which an empty pedestal, finally stripped of its Confederate relic statue, currently stands. The longer I live in Louisville, observing from a distance the wealth and power concentrated in that Triangle, the more I learn about the space between what stories tell us and what the record can show. Several houses have been believed, separately, to be the "true" Daisy home—the Moonie house, the Hilliard House, the old Emma Longest Moore home, each the designated pinnacle of twinkle-lit white wealth and malevolent carelessness in someone's yearning heart—and on each of those porches it is equally possible, on a warm spring evening, to glimpse from the sidewalk's safe distance a flash of streetlight reflecting off an unseen diamond. And if the actual model for her home is now believed to have been a house outside of Chicago where another rich white girl lived once upon a time? A muddled provenance just means Daisy, that ghastly apparition, should feel most at home in a city where she can be southern and midwestern all at once.

And I learned that downtown on the corner of Fourth and Walnut—a few steps from the Seelbach Hotel, Daisy's wedding reception venue, where I would later sit in communion with my Spalding University family of writers, those chosen cousins, some of whom are ghosts now too—is where the Trappist monk Thomas Merton had his famous epiphany, realizing that he loved the total strangers around him and could see the secret beauty of their hearts and would no longer shut himself away from the world. There's a historical marker commemorating the very spot of this spiritual revelation in front of an outdoor mall that hosts a never-ending rotation of corporate restaurants like, at the time of this writing at least, celebrity chef Guy Fieri's Smokehouse. When I stand on Merton's epiphany spot, I am reminded to feel just a bit warmer toward the people milling in the middle of the sidewalk, walking too slowly for my taste toward their overpriced reservation at Flavor Town.

And I learned that Walnut Street, once the business artery of Louisville's Black community before it caught the brunt of urban renewal's destruction, was the previous identity of the street now bearing the name of Muhammad Ali, whose Olympic medal I learned mingled with fossils at the bottom of the Ohio when young Cassius Clay chucked it off the Second Street Bridge after being refused service in a local restaurant after bringing the gold home. And I learned that the record can't show if that actually happened or if the city just collectively dreamed it, and while that wasn't my first lesson on the relationship between fact and truth, it is one that's stuck.

One thing I have learned from the poems and essays in this collection is that Louisville is a city bound by its contradictions as much as its alignments. Republican power broker Senator Mitch McConnell lives in Louisville next to the liberal neighbors who protest his policies on the sidewalk in front of his home. The city has been shaped by conservative seminarians and renegade punks, honkytonk bands and ravers, intentional activists and accidental movement leaders, church ladies and the families who park cars for cash in their front yards on Derby Day. (All of us, as Merton reminds me, walking around shining like the sun.)

There is no definitive Louisville, as I hope readers will see in the writing collected in this book, much of it personal and vulnerable, though undeniable threads of melancholy and resistance are woven across their different narratives. Some of the versions of the city reflected in this anthology no longer exist. Others are perhaps on their way to becoming artifacts, forever changed by a global pandemic forcing dramatic alterations to the ways we work, socialize, and learn; by the violence of gentrification; or by a movement of grassroots activists demanding justice for Black victims of police brutality and the city's systemic acts of racial and economic violence. What the Louisville that emerges from this era will look and feel like, we can't yet know.

And so I ask you to forgive this collection its limits; every Louisville that lives and breathes couldn't possibly be accounted for, let alone every Louisville that ever was or will be pressed into memory. Think of this as one limited, meandering tour of the city, with a few road trips outside its limits. Linger inside a beauty salon in Shively, a church talent show in Shawnee, a Butchertown mansion's fading elegance, the Brown Theatre, the Churchill Downs grandstands. Share a moment at the Pegasus Parade, at a Preston Highway red light, at a synagogue vigil, in an Okolona parking lot, on West Broadway as Derby cruisers line the street. Heed the altar call of Air Devil's Inn on a Saturday night. Stroll with us among the dead in Cave Hill Cemetery, take shelter from a tornado in a corporate craft store, test your wits against the city's most competitive bar trivia team. The difference between a right and wrong answer about a place often depends on who's asking. Every version of this city has and will hold its truths. "What other stories do I have yet to unearth about my homeplace?" Almah LaVon Rice asks in her essay. I know, as the story of Muhammad Ali's medal reminds me, there are always more buried deep, waiting for their persistent divers.

That Chekhovian Feeling of Living in the Provinces

EMMA APRILE

Magnolia, river birch, dogwood, sugar maple,
      redbud, Bradford pear:
Louisville smells like a place to come from,
      or a street's empty house,

its ivied sidewalk, from where we moved away.
      Pigeons—not doves—& gray
squirrels scatter across our landscape.
      One rabbit, dog-frozen

in an alley, too alert to run. Once, in summer's
      pigtails, I believed the future
opened like an ocean to carry us along.
      The high sweet sound

of an undiscovered soprano dissipates
      down by the Ohio.
Further north, empty Indiana hills metamorphose
      into elevation lines

of cornstalks, rows upon rows. Boy's
      hand on a glass, icy steps,
an ache after our father's black mustache
      turns white—each

sparkle catches my eye, that blue-hazed
      magpie. Which bauble
shall I turn out of my nest? Our future
      fills up with pastiche,

paste & glass, detritus of pauses, kisses,
          swallowed tears, a single
glazed eye. Who's to say the past constructs
          itself of anything else?

River's surge creeps in around us, buildings, coal barges,
          our own inevitable fog.
Time, you showman's house of cards,
          you jackdaw's nest,

turn yourself into distance, watch cars swoop away
          on the overpass—stretch out
your arms. Tell to us our own embellished stories
          of the once-full places,

all sepia & ivory, that we would one day say
          we came from. In the end,
gravity draws us back: our cosmic dust, asteroids ringing
          round this old collapsing star.

Strike City

RICHARD BECKER

Like many American cities, Louisville's landscape is dotted with abandoned factories, dilapidated warehouses, and overgrown, empty lots pockmarked with crumbling concrete pillars and brick edifices. On a foggy morning these hulking structures loom over the surrounding streets, silent reminders of the city's industrial past. This type of imagery is familiar to countless communities across the Midwest and Upper South. It is the imagery of deindustrialization, globalization, deregulation, or, to borrow a banal economists' term, "capital flight."

In these buildings, thousands of Louisvillians once labored, producing tractors, cigarettes, automobiles, and refrigerators. Now, save for a few large manufacturers like Ford and General Electric, most of these jobs are gone, replaced by a mix of low-wage service jobs, and jobs in logistics and healthcare.

Louisville is Kentucky's largest city. The curves of the Ohio River trace its border with Indiana. Early in the city's history, its location on the banks of the Ohio cemented it as the economic engine of the state. From its earliest days, Louisville was populated by a vibrant assortment of immigrants—particularly German, French, and Irish—who took up trades in manufacturing, river-boating, brewing, meatpacking, textiles, and other industries. These immigrants not only brought their work ethic, culture, and religious traditions; they also brought with them radical, militant politics.[1] The predominance of such values made the city's workers ripe for labor unrest as Louisville grew from a modest river town into a buzzing center of manufacturing and commerce.

The city's geographic and cultural status—is it midwestern or southern?—has long been the subject of considerable debate and friction among its denizens. The clash over which values should dominate the local economy and politics—a product, in part, of the city's unclear identity—can be seen in the city's rich labor history. Companies would locate factories in Louisville, assuming that, as a southern city, the risk of their workers organizing a union would be lower than in the heavily unionized north. But as we will see in the case of International Harvester, that was not a reliable assumption.

1 | See *German Influences in Louisville*, C. Robert Ullrich and Victoria A. Ullrich, ed. Charleston: The History Press, 2019.

I can't remember when I first heard the term "Strike City," but over the course of almost a decade of working as a union organizer in Louisville, I hear the term frequently. Depending on who is speaking, the words are uttered with derision (business leaders, conservative politicians), wistfulness (young labor militants or veterans of the era that gave rise to the phrase), or in a neutral tone, as when my father recalls the frequent strikes at General Electric's Appliance Park, about a mile from his childhood home. There are as well the labor leaders who in hushed tones chastise any fellow unionist who invokes the term, lest the specter of Louisville's militant past be used against us in today's never-ending deluge of anti-union attacks from corporate America and their politicians.

How Louisville became "Strike City"

From 1971 to 1980, Louisville saw more strikes and walkouts than any other major city in the nation, in spite of the fact that average worker pay at the time was higher than almost any other city in America, including the more affluent northern cities. In 1982, the Louisville *Courier-Journal* ran a three-part series investigating how Louisville came to be such a hotbed of labor unrest in the post-war era. These articles marked the first notable reference to the term "Strike City" to describe this medium-sized town on the Ohio River. The name stuck, and as the years passed, the moniker became an albatross around the neck of the city's economic development leaders.

In a front page story in the *Courier-Journal* on June 6, 1982 entitled, "Louisville's labor climate is chilly," journalist Jay Lawrence would set out to "counter the perception" that Louisville's strike-prone workers were giving the city a bad name with potential investors and stunting the region's economic growth. Noting that Louisville had lost nearly twenty thousand manufacturing jobs in the preceding decade, Lawrence concludes that the city's "labor climate" was indeed to blame for its economic woes. Through interviews with business and labor leaders, and an exhaustive analysis of government labor data, the paper sought to understand how Louisville had come to be known for labor strife, and what could be done to undo the damage that reputation had caused.

Lawrence seems almost incredulous that the city's workers—among the most well-paid in the South!—would ever even think of going on strike. This reaction ignores the apparent reality that it is precisely *because* of frequent strikes—and the implicit threat of more—that Louisville workers earned wages higher than fellow workers in the south. Far from being an argument against direct action, the piece strongly suggests that workers' unusually high level of activism paid off, quite literally. We see this not only in the *C-J*'s 1982 retrospective of the 1970s, but also in a chapter from earlier in Louisville's history, when the radical Farm Equipment Workers union took repeated, dramatic direct action to combat low wages and systemic racism at the city's International Harvester plant.

International Harvester and FE Local 236

When International Harvester acquired a former defense factory in Louisville in 1946, the company had high hopes for a productive facility to churn out three new models of tractors.[2] Given that this would be the company's first plant in the south, and that unionization levels were high elsewhere in its production pipeline, it stands to reason that IH sought a southern locale at least in part with the hopes of avoiding a union drive. Despite their best efforts, IH soon faced an organizing drive from the Farm Equipment Workers union (FE).

Having beaten the UAW and one other union in a contentious representation election in July 1947, Local 236 immediately went to battle with IH management over the company's "southern differential" pay rates. Under this pay system, Louisville's workers would be paid less than their counterparts at IH facilities elsewhere in the country. The confrontation eventually led to a walkout of Local 236's two thousand Louisville members. The strike lasted forty days before Harvester relented, offering sizable pay increases and handing the FE its second victory that year.

Labor historian Toni Gilpin extensively researched Louisville's FE Local 236 for her 2020 book *The Long, Deep Grudge*. Gilpin, whose father was an early leader in FE before its eventual absorption into the United Auto Workers (UAW) in the 1950s, writes of the successful strike of 1947, "From then on, the union relied on militant and immediate confrontation with management to protect workers interests."[3]

FE would not ride high for long, however. The radical union faced opposition not just from Harvester, but from within the labor movement as well. The United Auto Workers, headed by the charismatic Walter Reuther, began an aggressive takeover campaign against FE. This effort saw Reuther himself visit Louisville to personally make his pitch to FE members at International Harvester. Invoking the cooperative spirit developing between the UAW and the corporations whose workers it represented, and

2 | "1948 International Harvester Annual Report". International Harvester Company. 1949. Retrieved January 20, 2020.

3 | https://www.leoweekly.com/2015/09/strike-city-louisvilles-labor-legacy-and-future/

the stability that such a relationship engendered, Reuther promised that "by switching to the UAW such stability could become reality within International Harvester plants as well." [4]

Thus Reuther and his UAW shrewdly invoked the instability of walkouts, strikes, and other militant action—the very militant action that had won Louisville IH workers a huge pay increase—to persuade those same workers that they should trade the strength of their organization for the peace and stability enjoyed by members of the UAW. Though FE would continue for another half a decade to represent workers in Louisville and elsewhere, continued fierce resistance from Harvester combined with the specter of McCarthyism would injure the union severely enough that in 1955, FE relented and merged with the UAW. The merger was perhaps fitting, as the company had proclaimed in the early 1950s, "We don't have trouble with *labor*. We just have trouble with FE." [5]

Just a few miles from the International Harvester facility, General Electric's Appliance Park manufacturing facility experienced its own share of labor militancy. Ground was broken on the massive facility in 1951, with the plant opening in 1957. In the decades that followed, thousands of workers flocked to Louisville to work at GE, coming from across Kentucky and the region. At its peak, in 1972, Appliance Park employed 23,000 people, of which roughly 15,000 were union members. Employment numbers at the massive complex took a nosedive in the decades to follow, with the total number of workers today standing at around 6,000.

Ask any Louisvillian of a certain age, and they will likely be able to recall the labor turmoil that dominated headlines about Appliance Park in the post-war years. According to the 1982 *Courier-Journal* "Strike City" reports, General Electric alone saw 405,100 days lost to work stoppages in the decade spanning 1971-1980.

What allowed for such a frenzy of work stoppages was an unusual clause in the union contract. Under this clause, the union could call a strike not just over unfair labor practice charges or contract disputes during negotiations—the two most common strike justifications—but over individual workers' grievances. This meant that if a worker was terminated or disciplined over something the workers' deemed frivolous or unjust, the workers could shut down the plant and walk off the job, forcing the company to reverse the action. What's more, because this was in writing in the union contract, the company could not terminate or otherwise retaliate against workers who struck in such situations.

4 | Toni Gilpin, *The Long Deep Struggle*. Chicago: Haymarket Books: 2020, 190.
5 | Ibid, 4.

Today, very few people can remember the Strike City days firsthand. When I first began researching this essay and considering who I could speak to about this local history, two names immediately came to mind: Henri Mangeot and Herb Siegal. Mangeot served for years as the chairman of the Louisville Labor-Management Committee, spearheading the city's efforts to bring a more "cooperative" approach to labor relations. Siegel was a legendary union-side labor lawyer who represented hundreds of thousands of union members over the course of his sixty-plus year career. Both men—outsized figures in Louisville's labor history—are now deceased.

"Strike City" invokes a time of labor militancy in Louisville's history that has all but faded from the collective memory. The disappearance of this history owes partly to the natural disintegration that comes with time, and partly to a concerted effort by the city's business and civic leaders to "strike" this period from the record books in pursuit of "economic development" and "labor-management cooperation." In many ways, big business has won the "labor peace" promised by federal collective bargaining laws passed in the 1930s. Industry won its peace not through collaboration or cooperation, but through a mélange of outsourcing, contracting and sub-contracting, offshoring, and automation. Toss in a healthy dose of strategic, aggressive, and well-funded union-busting, particularly in the wake of President Reagan's firing of over ten thousand striking air traffic controllers (Louisville Standiford Field airport saw thirty-two controllers terminated for striking), and you have a recipe for a quiescent workforce.[6]

Two of the city's largest unionized employers—General Electric and Ford, represented by IUE-CWA and UAW, respectively—played an important role in re-shaping the city's image to be more friendly to corporate interests. GE for its part engaged in a massive "restructuring" in the '80s and '90s, which saw nearly ten thousand workers in Louisville lose their jobs. Ford has also phased down American production through offshoring and has pursued a strategy of cozying up to union leadership. Today's joint Ford-UAW newsletters represent a very different climate from the era of the Battle of the Overpass, a 1937 incident in which company thugs mercilessly beat union organizers at Ford's River Rouge Plant in Dearborn, Michigan.

Little more than a year after the *Courier-Journal* ran its "Strike City" series, the remaining seven hundred employees at International Harvester's Louisville foundry were laid off as the company announced the plant's permanent closure.

---

6 | "New Standiford route team settles into routine," Louisville Courier-Journal, August 20, 1981.

In spite of these losses, Louisville's labor movement presses on, in some ways unwittingly drawing inspiration from earlier generations of Strike City labor activists. 2017 saw a wildcat strike by dozens of construction workers at the future site of an Omni Hotel. In 2018, Kentucky teachers took a page from the West Virginia playbook and marched on their state capital, forcing the state's Republican legislature to back off proposed cuts to the state's public pension system. The effort was led by a coalition of teachers from the state's rural school districts as well as from the state's largest, in Louisville.

As Louisville moves deeper into the twenty-first century, the shortcomings of the city's "business-friendly" approach to public policy are increasingly laid bare. Low-wage service jobs and back-breaking logistics work continue to dominate employment in the city. With the teacher strikes, the Fight for $15 campaign, and the numerous direct actions by laid-off coal miners getting headlines, perhaps the workers of Strike City will remember and reconnect with their city's rich heritage of taking a walk when they're wronged by the boss.

Nobody's Home

ELLEN BIRKETT MORRIS

I hear the call, one voice:

Mr. Sessions has used the awesome power of his office to chill the free exercise of the vote by Black citizens in the district he now seeks to serve as a federal judge. This simply cannot be allowed to happen.

Then the response, many voices in unison:

Mr. Sessions has used the awesome power of his office to chill the free exercise of the vote by Black citizens in the district he now seeks to serve as a federal judge. This simply cannot be allowed to happen.

Light from cell phone screens illuminate clusters of people standing in the street. Around two hundred of us, young and old, parents and children, stand in front of our senator's condo. The road is blocked on either side by police cars.

Residents of nearby condos peek out of their windows nervously. We are a polite crowd. No one stands on the grass, and out of courtesy there are no bullhorns.

Mitch McConnell's condo is flat-faced, shades up, lights off, nobody home. McConnell offers the same lack of response to the letters we send him. His office phone number is busy. E-mails go unanswered. When he returns home to Louisville, McConnell is picked up on the tarmac so he can avoid protestors in the airport.

When McConnell defeated Senator Dee Huddleston in 1984, he ran an ad that showed bloodhounds trying to track down Huddleston in Washington, Los Angeles, and Puerto Rico. We could use those dogs today. Now, there are posters that superimpose Mitch's face on Lionel Richie's head with the message: *Hello, is it me you're looking for?*

I grew up in this neighborhood and live here still. McConnell's street led to the drugstore where I bought candy as a child. I played hide and seek among the trees that line this road. I lived here in the 1970s when there were public service messages about ecology on television; before the climate was so politicized that people would argue about pollution, even as they coughed into handkerchiefs. Louisville's pollution problem got worse, not better. Now we have "ozone action days" where children, the elderly, and people with medical conditions are urged to stay inside.

We were a segregated city in the '70s. We are a segregated city now with a record number of homicides in mostly African-American neighborhoods. The previous summer, people of all races filled the streets and stood shoulder to shoulder as we watched the motorcade carrying Muhammad Ali's body make its way through the city.

Ali's celebration was a moment of hope and unity. It is a tiny second in a long history of racial oppression, a legacy that runs so deep that I wonder if we will ever find reconciliation. Speaking out is a start. Standing up against the tide of hate and fear is a start.

I join the line to read. A young couple holding a baby read right before me. The mother's voice is strong and full of hope. She hands me the letter. I read:

Particularly in the South, efforts continue to be made to deny Black people access to the polls, even where they constitute the majority of the voters. It has been a long uphill struggle to keep alive the vital legislation that protects the most fundamental right to vote. A person who has exhibited so much hostility to the enforcement of those laws, and thus to the exercise of those rights by Black people, should not be elevated to the federal bench.

I hear the words echo back to me. We might be whistling into the wind, but the line of people wanting to read snakes down the block. The words bounce off the empty building and ring into the night.

We will remember this night. And we will vote.

Falls of the Ohio

BRENDA YATES

Rapids gouged, pried open the sea bed,
left it gaping at the sky. Now it's a river,
wide, and somewhat tame. From its edge,
time terraces up a steep slope like carved
stairs. Easily climbed. My hand spans
a million years of ocean floor. Polished
spirals and whorls shine in layer upon
layer of mud turned stone, calcified cross-
sections of top, side, inner chamber.
Further on, fossils jut from Devonian earth,
striations machine-tool perfect. A horn-
shaped piece loosens and comes away:
cornucopia of once living coral in my palm.
I carry its 400 million years to the clifftops,
where a thin coat of dust is not enough
to remember my footprints.

Good-Hearted Folks

BEN GIERHART

I pulled up in front of the garage door with a plea, "DON'T BLOCK THE GARAGE DOOR. PLEASE AND THANKS," tagged in black spray paint. My car's engine rumbled gently. I hadn't made the commitment to turn it off yet, so I sat there in front of the building on East Broadway idling a few moments, right behind my uncle's iridescent blue vehicle.

I heard a tap on the glass of my window and jumped a little, then saw that it was my uncle, smiling. He must have been waiting for me. When I stepped out and got a good look at him, I saw that he looked good today, especially considering what we had planned for the afternoon. He had a fresh haircut and beard trim, and he wore pressed khakis and a polo shirt that matched the color of his car and his eyes, though you couldn't see them with the sunglasses he was wearing.

"You look good, Uncle John," I said.

He seemed bemused by my observation. It was a happy accident, I guess. I thought of the infinite monkey theorem—the idea that a monkey hitting keys at random on a typewriter for an infinite amount of time will eventually replicate *Hamlet*.

"Do you like my sign?"

He meant the words on the garage door.

"Yeah. Should I move?"

"Nah. It's just us today. Besides, you're family," he said with a toothy grin.

We made our way to the front door. I noticed how the powerlines leading to the building had been cut and the scorch marks on its brick side. I saw the busted windows being held together by some sort of heavy-duty tape, and I saw the rusted window grills in front of them. I saw the way my uncle looked at all those things, too.

As we made our way to the front of the building, I spotted one of my favorite artifacts—a large electric sign, ingeniously created using the frame from one of those chalkboards on wheels they had in classrooms when I was growing up.

A jack of hearts, the traditional design from a set of playing cards, adorned the sign. It read, "Jack Heartt Company—Good Hearted Folks For Over 20 Years."

"Almost fifty now," I muttered, more to myself than anyone.

I was so excited to get out of school early. Already, Broadway was full to bursting. Roads were closed off, bleachers set up. My cousins and I sat on the sidewalk in office chairs commandeered from Jack Heartt for the afternoon, waiting for the Pegasus Parade to start, decked out in full regalia—party hats, sunglasses, Pegasus pins for the lucky ones. We thought we were sensational. We were.

"Papa, do you have more of those cookies?" asked one of my cousins.

I heard my grandfather before I saw him. He had a comically large set of keys hanging from his belt loop on a carabiner I had given him for Christmas the year before. I had been especially proud of that gift. He was always losing his keys, and he was a fervent devotee to the school of pragmatism. I had a tight budget, so this had been the best gift I could come up with. He wore his keys on his belt loop every single day from that day on.

Dressed in his usual uniform of coffee-stained shirt, grease-stained khakis, sunglasses that were actually protective eyewear for soldering, and a navy blue baseball cap emblazoned with the word "CAPTAIN," you couldn't say that my grandfather was anything short of a true original.

"Of course," he said, handing my cousin another box. He always had more. "Would you like some, Benjamin?" he added.

"Yes, please, Grandfather," I said. We were always so formal with each other.

After he stepped away, one of my cousins asked me, "Why don't you call him Papa like the rest of us?"

I had met my mother's mother years before her father. A true Southern belle, my grandmother insisted on nothing less than the full title. No grand-mas, meemaws, or mamies allowed. Grandfather had never taken himself so seriously. But I had spent the first ten years of my life in California, far away from Louisville where, unbeknownst to me, it was acceptable to call him Papa. When we finally met, I afforded him the respect I thought he desired. He never corrected me. That's simply what I called him, and no one else.

"I guess I just have my own name for him," I said with a shrug.

"I guess you're right. About fifty years," my uncle said, after a moment's thought.

We stared at the front door for a while, saying nothing. I stalled.

"How are the girls?" I asked.

"Oh, you know. One's in college. One's … staying with your aunt."

I knew this already.

"How's your mom?" he asked, though he knew that, too.

"She's doing the best she can," I said. I thought of something my grandfather said once.

More silence.

"Well, I guess we should get to work," he said, and without another moment's hesitation he opened the door.

Inside it looked exactly as it always had, which is to say it looked like a mess. Opened and unopened boxes alike littered the office, pages from ancient daisy-chain printers everywhere. I imagined we were witnessing the aftermath of some sort of obsolete office supply-themed rave. Somehow, inexplicably, I still smelled fresh-brewed coffee.

I spotted a box of cookies near a computer that looked to be older than I was. I walked over and looked inside the box; it was empty. Why was I so disappointed?

"I see Grandfather left his tools lying around," I quipped, gesturing toward the box.

My uncle roared with laughter.

"Here," he said, throwing some gloves and a paper safety mask at me. "We need this."

He launched into a scheme about selling some of the gloves at farmers markets. Truthfully, I was only half-listening. I kept marveling at how the inside of Jack Heartt looked exactly as I remembered. All the half-finished projects seemed like they were ready for my grandfather to just jump back in at any given moment. They yearned for tinkering.

"Anyway, that's not what we're here for," he said, "Come with me."

"OK."

"What did you say?"

"You've got to speak up!" he said.

"Attention!" I screamed, wiping tears from my eyes.

We were in the middle of an open field in a park somewhere. I don't know which one. I had just come from Taekwondo practice, and I was still dressed in my uniform.

"Grandfather, I hate it."

"You hate what?" he said with his hand to his ear.

"I hate Taekwondo! I'm not any good at it!"

"That black belt you're wearing tells a different story."

"I'm just good at memorizing things… I'm too quiet. And Master Juong

is so mean. He wants me to be louder when leading the class through exercises, and I'm really trying. It's not fair."

"Do you want to be quiet?"

"Sometimes."

"All the time?"

"…No."

"Why?"

I stared at him in disbelief, barely suppressing silent sobs.

"People pick on me."

"I know," he said matter-of-factly, and upon some reflection he added, "When I was in the Army, I had to be a leader sometimes. Sometimes when I didn't want to be."

My ears perked up. My grandfather didn't talk about his time in Korea very often. It had never occurred to me until that moment that he had that history and he was helping me learn a Korean martial art.

"Why didn't you want to be a leader?"

"It's a lot of responsibility, for one," he said, "And I was like you. I liked joking with the guys, not being in charge. I was quiet when I had to do that."

"I didn't know that."

"Well, you were born very young." It was one of his catchphrases. I laughed. "Try again," he said. "I know you can do it."

I mustered everything I had and let it rip: "Attention!"

It was a coincidence, I know, but I swear all the dandelions in that field blew apart in that moment and floated off into the sky—off to fill a new field and challenge another little boy.

I cleared my throat and spoke up. "I just said OK. Let's go."

I followed my uncle into the back of the building. This was uncharted territory for me. None of the grandchildren had been allowed in the back when we were kids, and it was easy to see why. This was where my grandfather kept his serious pet projects. He was a maniac for cars and various oddities of engineering. I imagined the cars intact, coming to life only to stumble around with a violent flu and spew their guts. I was so distracted by this thought that I nearly walked into a pile of tools and tripped. For a safety equipment business, this part of Jack Heartt sure seemed to be a hazard.

"Careful," said my uncle. "That would have hurt."

"That looks like it hurt," he said.

"Not too much," I said cavalierly. "Where's Mom?"

"She's upstairs with your grandmother."

"Is she OK?

"She will be. I'm going to take some pictures now, OK?"

"Why?"

"I want to make sure there's some evidence in case the police don't do it. Take a step back and point out where he hit you."

He pulled a Kodak disposable camera from his pocket, and I idly wondered what else was on that camera. What reel of memories would I be ruining? Which shocked photo developer would see the vacation photos or whatever that abruptly shifted into evidence of child abuse?

We took several photos, some gesturing to the sore spot under my eye and on my cheek. It was already raised. There would be a hard lump there for a while.

When we were finished, I said, "He said stuff about me. And Mom."

"I know."

My hands were shaking. "He said things that weren't true. He said stuff about Uncle John and Aunt—he said stuff about you."

"I know."

"We were Taekwondo training in the basement. And he started saying things, and ... I was so mad. I love my family, and he was saying mean things. I couldn't listen anymore. I had to say something because it wasn't right ... and he punched me in the face."

It was only the second time I'd told that story and I already recited it, dis- associated, cold. I doubted myself. Even with a throbbing pain and lump on my cheek and under my eye I wondered if it had really happened.

And then I worried that it had. I started to cry.

"Why didn't Mom do anything earlier?"

He was quiet again for a long time. "Sometimes when your mother has made a mistake, it's difficult to make her realize it."

I didn't know what to say. "If they get a divorce, it'll be my fault."

"It's not your fault."

"It is. If I hadn't told Mom about what happened ... and what's happened before, she wouldn't have brought us here and the police wouldn't be coming."

Ages passed.

"Sit down."

I did.

"Listen to me. It is not. Not. Your fault. You did a very brave thing."

I was crying again.

"A very brave thing, and I'm very proud of you. You just saved your mother.

You saved me from worry. You saved yourself. You did what needed to be done and what no one else did. Whatever happens now is what needs to happen, and it will happen because you were brave."

I kept crying. I was a fountain on a rooftop. When my pipes were finally dry, I asked, "How long will we stay here?"

My grandfather wasn't a believer in hugs, but he did touch my shoulder. It felt like a hug anyway. "As long as you need to."

"Be careful," said my uncle. "We've got as much time as we need."

I sheepishly walked out of the mess of tools and parts I'd stepped in and finally made it to our destination. The very back part of the building: the garage.

I imagined we were stepping into an alternate dimension where the laws of physics didn't apply. Like in a science fiction movie: colors heightened, objects in impossible formations, structures standing that shouldn't be.

When I stepped out of my reverie, I saw part of the roof had collapsed. Even more parts of cars and computers were strewn everywhere. Floating detritus from a ravaged universe.

We were watching the 2009 Star Trek *movie, the one with Chris Pine and Zachary Quinto. It was a hot summer day, and we were enjoying some much-needed air conditioning after some family event, a Fourth of July or Memorial Day cookout. My grandfather was a big* Star Trek *fan but hadn't seen this one. I lobbied heavily for it to be the movie we all watched together.*

"I didn't think that Spock was a very good Spock," said my aunt.

"He was one of my favorite parts," I replied more than a little defensively.

A cousin groaned. But I was having a great time. The movie was fun and action-packed. It was joyous to see the original series depicted in such a modern way with my grandfather, who had introduced me to Star Trek *in the first place.*

And then the scene happened.

In an early part of the movie, Spock, played by Zachary Quinto, is speaking with the Vulcan High Council. I distinctly remember thinking then about how impressive I thought his performance was. A love letter to Leonard Nimoy yet also completely his own.

The camera zoomed in on his face.

"He is wearing so much eyeliner," said one of my cousins who wasn't a sci-fi fan.

"He looks like a fag."

My grandfather said it. And the entire room went silent, like we were all eradicated from existence after a bomb had been dropped. I don't remember how it went back to normal because for me, the rest of the movie didn't happen.

Up until the credits rolled, all I saw was the man who had given me cookies at the Pegasus Parade for years, who had taught me to find my voice, who had comforted me when I had used it, who had taught me the virtue of patience and the benefits of thoughtfulness, that man had called me a fag.

He hadn't. He'd called an openly gay actor, one that many people had told me I looked like, a fag. And there wasn't a person in that room who didn't know what that comment had done to me, but no one said a word.

When it was finally time to go, I raced out the door.

The garage door with the spray-painted words was broken. I could see that the apparatus that allowed it to be opened was busted.

"What happened?" I asked.

"There was a fire. Electrical surge outside the building, and part of it made its way inside. Nothing too bad. The fire department got here pretty quickly."

My uncle paused for a second. He was angry.

"So they broke the garage door?"

"Getting in. Yeah."

"And now we have to clean it up."

"Yeah."

"At least we have something to clean up," I said looking around at the mess. Only a small part of it was caused by the fire. The rest had just been there.

"Why did Grandfather let it get so bad in here?"

"Papa just ran out of time," said my uncle. He took his sunglasses off, and I saw a look in his eyes. I imagined diving into the iridescent pool of his irises. I recalled the last time I had seen him look like that.

"I'm sorry to say that… He did die."

It was the middle of the night. My mom had gotten a call that my grand-father was in the hospital and that she should come. That it was serious. My grandfather had had some health issues for the past year or so. I'm a notoriously heavy sleeper, but for some reason that call woke me, and I went with my mom to the hospital.

My grandmother, uncle, aunt, and my mom were all there. We had waited for a long time, and we were finally ushered into what turned out to be the Bad News Room.

When my uncle heard, he wailed. That's the only acceptable word for it.

"He died in my arms," he cried.

That turned out not to be hyperbole. I learned later that my grandfather's heart had given out and that my uncle had tried to revive him, all the way to the hospital and again at the hospital.

"I'll give you all a moment in your grief," said the doctor.

We sat there in stunned silence. The door opened again.

"Can any of you spare a couple bucks?" asked a strange man. There was a teeter to his gait and a slur in his speech that indicated he was pretty drunk.

I realized that I actually recognized him. I didn't have a car, so I rode the TARC everywhere. There's a community of bus riders in this city, and I knew him by sight. One time he had asked if I would play Snoop Dogg on my phone for us to listen to. I don't know if I did it because I was afraid or because I thought it would be funny, but I played "Who Am I (What's My Name)" for us both on the bus that day.

"What do you want the money for?" I asked him.

My family stared at me in disbelief.

"I just want something from the vending machine," he said, completely oblivious to what he had interrupted.

"All right. Come with me. I'll get you whatever you want."

I found a nearby vending machine. He picked out a couple things he wanted, and I had just enough cash to pay for it. "God bless you," he said on his way out, clutching his prizes.

"You too," I said, and I walked my way back into the Bad News Room, into the impossibility.

My grandmother said something about how my grandfather had always given money to the poor, and that he must have been with me just now. But I'd never felt less like he was with me than I had felt in that moment when I learned that he died.

"He just ran out of time," my uncle said.

"Why has no one else gone in here since he died?" I asked.

"Too painful."

I imagined my grandfather in the garage, cleaning and repairing, moving like high-speed camera footage of the weather. I imagined him fixing all the cars, the roof now intact. Every mote of dust, every dried speck of oil lifted. The garage returned to its former state. I tightened my mask, pulled up gloves, and walked to the garage door. We had work to do. I saw what the place could be with a little elbow grease from a couple of good-hearted folks. We went to work.

Too Bad the Whole World Swings Metal

DEREK MONG

for Heather Slomski

and not big league wood, which splinters
                                    into on-field
shards, but sings truer than aluminum. Just catch a college
game: those lineups form
                          like tuning forks in search of music.
Then there's Louisville. The Slugger Plant. Here dudes heft
wood replicas—
                I gripped Babe's handle, knob, and sweet spot.
Funny that. No quick-tongued teen, no ex-jock dad
addresses the entendre,
                          each returned to the foul lines
and pitcher's mound that once bound all ambition.

Still, I'm mid-stroke before I recall
                                    the last full swing
taken by my best friend's cousin when he punched out
a nurse after waking (post-op)
                                to find himself one nut
shy of a swing-set. I'd laugh were he not spared cancer
of the crotch, and serving
                            six to ten in cinderblocks
for a fear which (in the slang of gunslingers and dugouts)
any swinging dick
                    would vouch for. You've known it too,
or half of you. It's why we balk at neutering our pups

and provide cups for T-ball.
                            And by high school
the game that keeps no time becomes a metaphor
for touching women.

With Jill he dove like Pete Rose for third.
Erin swore second was only a late inning option.
Both guys knew they were running
                                  home ad infinitum
though none foresaw what it'd be like to stay there:
lawn mowers idling beside deck chairs.
                                  Bases that fold up
like napkins. Guy friends watch them run the last

ninety feet, peering
                      from their dugouts like groundhogs.
They cannot see the one who awaits them with open arms—
who will embrace
                  the sweet earth still clinging to their jersey.

Preston Highway

ANDREW VILLEGAS

University gives way silently to those llanteras, carnicerias,
el mercados that hoist home from my stomach, fill my belly
with familiarity to sustain. The smell of packaged sweets, those

conchas on the side keep me: We aren't alone in a place
like this, we just have to drive to it. We grew in two worlds
accepted by none. My brother never visited me in this place, too

white, too southern midwest, nothing to offer. He knew better
than I what was here and I either lived in denial or hope
that acceptance came from living among them, driving

to express myself. It may be truly safer in Germantown, or I
have eaten sustainably long enough, walked to the ice cream shop
times uncountable to tell myself: There is no one like me; that's how

it should be. The haunts, the faces, familiar acceptance lies in mute
ladybugs hanging from blades of grass. Call me in to sit. Make me
believe it won't always be this way. There's always someone

in the pipeline; we care. Somewhere along some road, it made me
feel special. I didn't need that part of me, better if it is tucked away
in Colorado. Better if the lid stayed on the pot of beans. Better safe

than packed three to a room. Better than poverty, than hunger, than fate.
The soothing side of me ¼ my blood, conquistadored, saved, made to
sign
the cross, ashed, filled with Jesus' love. On that road down, my heart beat

out accordion windows down, radios up and slicked punk rock back
home past the tire shops, the butcher, the market. Named safe at last,
locked
away, neighbors nervously watching my front door as I walk up the steps.

Running Red Lights

ANDREW VILLEGAS

Between city streets you ignored — parents, for generations
— the tires hugged, I recalled: You abandoned resolve.

Slick the new tread deep to rutting snow. In fall, trampled
weeds blew humidity straight off the ground, stuck

to backs peeled off and goosebumped. There's no point trying
to slow on melted snow, so I started running reds

too like Portland, like Lyndon, like St. Matthews, safer the more
Brownsboro Road I drove, the patron saint of a level playing field,

and knew time to leave.
                    The difference between

arriving two minutes before I would otherwise left choice: Keep
pedaling to ground and see where I go—inevitably twisted

fenders would need repair—or jab at brake, wait, change
tune, fidget before green, and turn down dark hair-pinned roads

widening east to suburb, the safe Kroger, where ice cream
doesn't melt. Where I walked the aisles to cure, late

nights, under the gaze of those who knew that walk signaled Other.
There the collards blanched in plain water,

no pork fat, no ham.
                    Our brains signal not thinking thoughts of red, mindlessly

considering rain depth, distance, pressure and time. Our feet do
the talking we won't: Accelerate, stop, check the brakes.

Our hands do the steering: Hold tight, turn smooth. For some
it's the push through, the matter matters not. Preservation

of independence tendered absolves self through reds: There,
I've done what I can, the man can't keep me down.

For others, automatic takes foot, slides to brake, the dull yellow
glow hammering corneas puffy: Others will run the lights I didn't need to.

"Blue Becomes You": An Ars Poetica

ASHA L. FRENCH

1.

There is a story my father told over and over, with both his living and dying breath. It is the story of "Blue becomes you," the three-word sentence my great-grandmother Lucy told my father, her first grandson, on a day that he never forgot. In so doing, she became the first American-born woman in the French line to compliment a dark-skinned grandboy. Her mother-in-law had bequeathed to her husband the color complex handed to her by unnamed relatives on a plantation in Athens, Alabama, but Grandma Lucy wasn't one to carry things that weren't her own (except for children), so she told my father how blue became him, which helped him become less blue about being called "crow feather" black. Then he married a cinamo-hogany woman and dreamed of having a deep brown daughter to tell that every color became her "just like her Daddy's" skin, but when I came out yellow and purple he cried anyhow and told the story of the way Grandma Lucy turned a crow into a prince a thousand times.

2.

Aunt Jean, my grandfather's little sister, named her daughter Lucy so she would always have a reason to say her gone mother's name and even though the naming did not reverse the curse that met us on these shores—the one where special people cross the water in their early forties, before they teach you how to recognize yourself as your own best thing—it did work to bridge the gap between this world and the next when all the little cousins Young Lucy loves learned the story of her name.

3.

One story of Young Lucy's name is that she was named after the girl-woman who married at just thirteen years old and fled from Athens to Louisville when "Bammas" started acting like the Confederacy never fell. By the time she'd found out Louisvillians weren't much more evolved, she'd already anchored herself to the city with babies so she made it home anyhow.

4.

Grandma Lucy left this plane when she was only as young/old as my big brother, who left me before I got to thank him for everything he'd helped me become. Like my brother, Grandma Lucy didn't leave too soon on purpose. What she left behind: these typing hands that my father's people hold and say "just like Mama's."

5.

It's 1988 and Grandma Lucy's grandkids and the grandkids of all the other just-like-family she made in this city are still meeting in the church she and her husband built on the corner of 41st and Vermont. Just look at all them new babies looking just like their way-back-kin singing "This Little Light of Mine" at the talent show, thereby getting the kind of vaccination our kids need for the diseases common on this side of the Atlantic.

6.

I think I am always talking about water when I tell you how a poet becomes a poet. I once wrote, "I remember my Grandma Lucy as a water song/humming 'live, daughter, live'" and my writing teacher in Bloomington, Indiana said she didn't understand the image and "what is a water song anyway" and "this feels like a first draft" and "it's rather pedestrian" as if she'd never swam in an amniotic sack. I didn't have the Lucy stories I needed back then to deflect these comments as the unbridled desire to pretend we didn't all come cross the water—some of us to destroy, others to resist destruction. And this teacher who publishes poetry about her dog's balls couldn't have known about my congenital heart defect or the prayers of Grandma Lucy's kin or the way I probably had heard that song seeing as how I was born alive anyhow and ain't woke up dead yet.

7.

This was supposed to be about that fateful church talent show in which I nervously recited a Shel Silverstein poem about a messy room and everybody cheered and then my big cousin, Young Lucy, showed me what poetry can really be—what it can help one become. I'm sure this wasn't the first time she held me but perhaps this is the first time she held me with words, voice, and Black girl style, or perhaps it was the first time I noticed that she was as tall as the stories of my great grandmother's spirit and I knew the words coming out of her mouth were the kind I wanted to write. The thought had to sit for thirty years to become what it is today but when

Cousin Lucy says, "I will be reciting a poem from Ntozake Shange's *For Colored Girls Who Have Considered Suicide/ When the Rainbow Is Enuf*," it is the first name other than my brothers' that I recognize as African—both familiar and out of place. It is the first time I know an American girl with an African name can write words that reach church basements miles away from New York City, which is only the center of some folks' universe and didn't have to be the center of mine.

8.

This is not to trace my literary heritage to Ntozake Shange the way Morrisonian scholars want to tell you she studied "classics" at Howard but don't want to tell you about Chloe Wofford's kinfolks or the way church folks saying, "Take your time, Baby" inevitably shaped her long sentences as much if not more than the Faulknerian prose she read for filth in a master's thesis about the way Blackness shows up especially when somebody is trying really hard to hide it. Rather, I am trying to unhide my kin from my own literacy story—tell you the way I learned everything I will ever need to know about what writing can do that night in the basement of Grandma Lucy's church.

9.

What good are words if I can't describe how Cousin Lucy's neck swivel sent the church into a shout when she said, "One thing I don't need/ is any more apologies/ I got sorry greetin me at my front door/ you can keep yours"?

10.

Word has always had to bow to spirit. The best of the pen wielders try hard to describe what it feels like to bloom at break-neck speed to the chorus of "Amen." But still, words fail to become that moment. I can only describe for you the reverb of Cousin Lucy's thunder or the shape of my head thrown back in wonder.

11.

Here is a theory I haven't confirmed because I'm not yet the cousin my father was so I don't always ask all the things I want to know: I think Cousin Lucy chose to recite "Sorry" because it resonated with the other Lucy in her blood—a feisty woman who had heard her share of "sorry" crammed into forty-three short years. A woman whose short life prepared her to giggle at "I'm not goin to be nice,/ I will raise my voice,/ & scream & holler/ & break things & race the engine/ & tell all your secrets bout yourself to your face…" I think it was Grandma Lucy who arranged for me to be in the room with her namesake to hear this particular poem so I could one day write myself to the realization that the most abusive, "sorry" lover is the failed project of American democracy. That knowing informs church folks' amen. What other devil are they rebuking once a week and sometimes twice?

12.
DuBois's double consciousness doesn't exist in the basement of a family church where nobody is preaching the sermon that will reinforce respectability and everybody is pouring into the next generation's torch bearers.

13.
One of my Lucys lit my torch with her hands on her hips, her neck rolling this way and that. From her I learned to leave space for "Amen," to let words rain until they are enough to sustain a fish out of water. My other Lucy has always been a water song humming, "I live, daughter. I live." She has shown me the alchemy of words—how a compliment becomes a grandson's favorite gift, how a grandson becomes his daughter's favorite man, how a great-granddaughter becomes a story keeper, carrying something blue in the water around her heart.

The Wiz Live from The Brown Theatre, Louisville, KY, December 2018

IDRIS GOODWIN

When *The Wiz* came to Louisville Black folk showed up
We donned our best to sing along to the songs
for songs we deem ours will forever be sacred

When *The Wiz* came to Louisville we remembered the time
we first saw Michael crucified in makeup and straw
his voice indistinguishable and possibly higher than Diana's
Nipsey Russell all silver and in his feelings

We remembered our uncles and aunties and cousins
belting and humming *Ease on Down*

So, when we heard *The Wiz* was coming to Louisville we paid
and it wasn't cheap, but this is sacred and at the classy Brown theater no less
and it stars Shirley Murdock, as the tradition of Black shows dictate

The play must star an R&B singer of eras past
like any self-respecting child of Motown
we shelled out the dough and we paid for the parking

Sat down, and of course they played Erykah Badu's live album, as we waited
while a brother made his way down the aisles selling programs
for five dollars we realized what this was going to be

Not *The Wiz* of our childhood, with Billboard's best and brightest
this would be the kind that sold programs for five dollars

The curtain will go up twenty minutes late
revealing a stage naked save for a confused actor and
an empty projection surface, and in that moment, you know
no tornado coming to sweep us away

No tornado came to sweep us away that Sunday at 3 p.m.
Just a collective groan, a wave across our chest
that time, like Michael's mind, gone

We forgot that at the end of the film Richard Pryor steps
out behind the wall
face bloated from the reckless '70s
no giant but a mere man with imagination

In the end *The Wiz* was a con
(not that we stayed 'til the end)
As swiftly as we bought tickets we retreated
eager as Dorothy's ruby heels

Tornado Warning/ JoAnn Fabric & Craft

MARTHA GREENWALD

—*There is desire & there is experience*
says the sales manager, his speech mock
thespian beneath the siren-laced gales—

Swayed by last weekend's empowerment seminar,
he's just called Corporate to quit. Thus after Valentine
rush, farewell to the service alcove where we shelter;
farewell quilters, O exiles of the pattern workshop.
Watery Gregorian chants sound in the walls & wind

regurgitates up fountain pipes, yet the quilters
refuse to be comrades in fear; humorless, calmly
thumbing calico squares stacked on their laps.

A bully mother has sent me, again, to fetch supplies
for her holiday class party. In my basket—25 pairs
of Googly Eyes. All parents will receive awkward
crimson hearts that blink in surprise at our boredom.
The manager rests his head on bolts of jade toile,

already gone to study costume design, four cities away.
Unseasonal storms dare not upset this fabric's pastoral:
shepherds court maidens, lutes forgotten in the meadows.

Consignment

AMY J. LUECK AND DAVID JAMES KEATON

I had a really hard time finding a wedding dress. As often is the case with many of my purchases, I was trapped between perfectionism and abject cheapness. I insisted that I didn't really care, mostly because I didn't want to spend the money it required to care about such things. So when a friend purchased a white dress for me at Zappos, a shoe outlet just outside of Louisville, I was determined to make it work. It was an inexpensive satin, A-line dress with an empire waist, wide satin straps, and a thin, sheer, sequined ribbon at the waist. It was a decent dress, I guess. But I didn't love it. It wasn't "special," like I had come to expect it would be. It hung sadly in my closet for months as I imagined ways to spruce it up with fabric flowers or a little jacket of some sort. But in the end, it was just a bit too simple and cheap, exactly the kind of dress you might find at a shoe outlet.

I bought another dress for my wedding and decided to consign the old one at B Chic, an absolutely chaotic consignment store in an old converted house on Bardstown Road. The place was packed floor to ceiling with clothes, shoes, and housewares, all on consignment, and the sense of overwhelmedness it produced was matched only by the manic energy of the clerk who most often oversaw the place. Her enthusiasm for each item revealed how they would have amassed such a collection.

This place was practically in our backyard at the time, as we were renting the second floor of a historic building whose address was on the idyllic Cherokee Road but whose backyard opened into a rowdy alley and a McDonald's parking lot, where we'd shamefully grab breakfast on the most desperate weekend mornings. I went to B Chic often to buy or sell clothes—but mostly to sell, as I had come off of a deceptively lavish retail-and-loan-funded lifestyle in my master's program smack dab into a much leaner, stipend-funded PhD program, which meant selling off all manner of unnecessarily expensive clothes and accessories I had accumulated. This is also why I began hosting trivia.

Which nineteenth-century prince popularized the exchange of snake-shaped engagement rings in Victorian England after he proposed to his queen-to-be with an emerald-headed serpent?

My fiancé and I had been doing pub trivia each week with friends from my program. Our team was called the Senile Felines, a palindrome we settled on after brief stints as the Taco Cat, Go Hang a Salami I'm a Lasagna Hog, and other similarly irritating reversible phrases. Since all of us were future crazy cat ladies with a mathematical average of two cats per household (so far), this was the name that stuck.

And we weren't too bad at it. Despite all being one-time English majors, we all had very different skills and areas of expertise. My future husband has always had a *Rain Man*-like memory for film (combined with Rain Man's brother's ill-fated money-making schemes), and his brain was so well-engineered for trivia competitions that he often rattled off extra unwanted trivia even more obscure than what was asked for. Others in our team had fairly comprehensive knowledge of books and movies, U.S. presidents, sports history, and, strangely enough, one was a self-declared Texas expert, who seldom answered a Texas question correctly, which was about the most Texas thing she could do actually. But she really brought it on late-'90s sitcoms. Oh, and me. I kept score really well.

So, instead of marriage counseling, my soon-to-be husband and I spent our nights preparing for marriage by observing one another in this special form of intellectual (if often drunk) teamwork, which seems like as good a preparation for marriage as any. Our favorite place to flex our collective brain muscles and win free grub was Zanzabar, a tiny music venue in Germantown lined with dozens of vintage pinball machines. There, the long-suffering trivia host spun the perfect mix of just-hip-enough music to accompany the addictive but heartburn-inducing tater tots, bone-dry sandwiches, and very strong local taps. We were sick every week from the grease and beer infusion, and yet there we were each Sunday to do it all again. We just couldn't resist the fact that our previously useless knowledge could not only win free bar food, but actual *money* money. Every team threw in one dollar per person, and the winning team took the pot. And on just the right summer night, this could amount to more than a hundred dollars, which was big money to us at the time, even if we had to split the pot a half dozen ways, and we spent three times that much on beer while trying to win. It all had about the same logic as buying a bunch of expensive clothes and then consigning them for half their value.

But Zanzabar wasn't the only local trivia we hit up. Mondays was trivia at the Bard's Town (on Bardstown!)—a much tougher crowd, but

you could get Shakespeare-themed fries while you lost. Tuesdays you could catch one at Mulligans, the since-closed Irish pub on Newburg with a sign inviting passing drivers who couldn't stop in to wave as they passed (something that still happened after it shut down). Wednesdays we even went so far as to venture into a dreaded Buffalo Wild Wings, where you could almost guarantee winning some hot wings and floppy celery in the midst of their overwhelming television wallpaper (almost always set to the wrong aspect ratio). So almost any night of the week, we were up and down Bardstown Road, making money—by which I mean, funneling money into food and alcohol, then getting most of it back in the form of vouchers for future refreshments. We were like the worst money launderers of all time.

Our plan was particularly flawed by the fact that other teams ran this circuit, too. Like us, they went around to all the trivia spots knowing they could destroy the casuals competing with them. The worst/best of them was called "Sexual Chocolate," consisting of a mean-looking bearded guy, his red-haired wife, and an old, gray dude who I think was her father? Or maybe it was his father. Either way, they dominated most places they went, and their dominance was all the more egregious given their small team size. They were our nemesis (probably everybody's nemesis), practically taking the beer right out of our mouths each week with their obscure knowledge of varied historical uses of snakes.

What is the actual title of Wagner's wedding processional commonly known in the U.S. as "Here Comes the Bride"?

It was at BW3 of all places that I first got the idea to level up from the precarious six-way-split as a trivia player to the big cash money: Trivia Host. Having spotted a busy young woman buzz into the bar one night to give some kind of instruction to a visibly hungover host, I approached her to ask if she managed the games and if she needed any help. And the next thing I knew, I was picking up trivia answer booklets and a stack of speakers and driving to my first gig one week later. It was a fun job. Not only did I pull in an extra hundred bucks each week to help ease the burden of grad-school living and wedding costs, but I also got to do it while hanging out in bars in front of a microphone, playing DJ for a room full of people while I told them over and over again that they were wrong. It was a dream come true, and the perfect catharsis after a long day of teaching, which was almost the exact mirror image of my moonlighting side hustle.

I began working several trivia shifts a week all around town. I picked up the shift at Mulligans for several months before they closed, then moved on to DiOrios on Baxter, where I got to enjoy the best pizza around but perhaps the worst bartender—a smooth-talking ex-surfer type whose charms had clearly overshadowed his incompetence for much of his life. In the winter, I grabbed a second shift when Maddios opened on Grinstead Road, which was on the same block as our house and made things even easier.

Maddios was a new pizza place with an over-lit, fast-food ambience, where you ordered at the counter, got a buzzer, and then sat in sculpted plastic chairs to await your food. You got your soda from one of those new soda machines that offered every imaginable soda and flavoring combination. It was very tidy but a far cry from the vibe of my other trivia bars. Their logo was even a clean red circle that looked corporate in just the wrong sort of way. I heard they're no longer there, which is some comfort since so many of our favorite places and people have also long since gone.

I hosted trivia at Maddios on Tuesday nights from a booth among the other patrons, there being no stage or even a good corner where I could post up with my microphone and music. Most people were surprised that trivia was offered in a restaurant like this, as it seemed more like a middle-school hangout. And to add insult to injury, my job there also required some heavy recruitment and salesmanship, trying to entice beleaguered families and confused couples to stick around a few extra hours after their meal for the prospect of earning another. The takers were few, with the exception of one or two teams of regulars, like (groan) Sexual Chocolate, who saw the blood in the water among this particularly unpracticed bunch.

I'd been working at Maddio's for a couple months when she came in. I was setting up for a show—stacking up the little notepads of answer slips, arraying out the game sheets, rifling through my bag for extra pens, and getting ready to solicit players from among the dead-eyed diners—when in walked a man in a humble suit, an older woman in jeans and a sweatshirt, and a young woman in a wedding dress.

What color wedding dresses did ancient Athenian brides traditionally wear?

I recognized the dress immediately.

It was the same dress I'd consigned at B Chic the month before. The tall, thin woman wearing it was younger than me, but somehow already older, if that makes any sense. Her hair was in a modestly styled updo, and her tattooed arms were bared to the mild Louisville winter. Her group ordered their pizza at the counter, filled their sodas, and sat down to await their meal. I watched them as they sat, not really talking to one another, and I contemplated what to do. Do I mention it? Of course not, right? But with a coincidence like that, how could I not? I was instantly aware of the power I had to make her feel shitty, if I played it wrong, and this responsibility had me frozen. I knew my desire to share what I knew, to identify the dress, was about me, not her. But I also knew I wouldn't be able to resist.

Eventually, I approached the group with a smile and told them about our trivia game.

"Do you guys want to play trivia?" I chirped. "We have a game starting at 7 p.m. It's free and you can win house cash!"

They conferred with one another and then said, "Sure, why not!"

Before I could stop myself, I said, "I'm sorry, but I have to ask, is today your wedding day?"

"Yep, we just got married!" the bride announced proudly to her new husband, as much as to me, and he responded with a quiet, slumping nod as if to say that all was well.

"Congratulations! You look beautiful." I filled the air with compliments and chatter almost compulsively, unsure what to do with myself and somehow unable to do nothing. Then, "Where did you get your dress?"

I knew I shouldn't have asked it as soon as it came out of my mouth. It felt rude. It *was* rude, given that I knew the answer and knew the position I was putting her in by asking it. Not to mention that it would have been impossible to explain my connection to her and the dress. Or how it had led me back to it, in its own strange way.

"Actually, I got it at the consignment store up the street. I love that place."

"Oh my god," I blurted out, somehow surprised to hear her confirm what I had already known. "That was my dress! I consigned it there!" I immediately regretted saying it, feeling certain she could read in my eyes all the negative things I had thought about that dress and knowing that the question of why I had sold it was floating between us.

"I bought it for my wedding this fall, but it never looked right on me. It looks beautiful on you, though," I insisted. "It was made for you."

I was frantically trying to recover from my stupid prying and exposure of her, to make it better. But the thing is, she didn't have a problem. She smiled coolly and was unaffected, even by the occasional red pizza stain on her dress as the night went on. Apparently, her wedding had been a simple ceremony at the courthouse and her reception, here at Maddios right in front of me, was even more so. I could not imagine it, but she was clearly happy with the whole affair. She even accepted the nervous trivia host trying to insert herself into her big day.

All night I played wedding and love-themed songs. "Endless Love," "My Girl," "Love Shack," even Tony! Toni! Toné!'s "All My Love." I also announced the couple's recent nuptials to the room (as if a woman in a wedding dress wasn't obvious enough), and we all cheered and celebrated— even Sexual Chocolate, though a bit begrudgingly, possibly annoyed they weren't the center of attention for once.

I was desperate to make it a good night, to make her feel special. But my interest was into my own story, not hers.

I wish I could say they won the trivia game that night, but they didn't. I'm not sure if they got a single question right, and they left before the game even ended, but I slipped her some vouchers anyway.

I watched her go and thought about celebrating my wedding with a quiet meal at the local pizza pub, instead of our museum ceremony three states away, and I was surprised to discover a new emotion regarding my discarded dress: jealousy.

I quit hosting trivia a few weeks later, and laughed to my husband that it was out of fear of more of my consigned clothing stalking me along the parade of bars on Bardstown Road and forcing me to confront my lingering uncertainties about their surrender. And I still think of her in my dress, and their unassuming celebration, more than my own ceremony.

Sourcewater: A Prosaic Sonnet

ALMAH LAVON RICE

I.

My mother bent at the white girl's feet, pinning. I'd seen my seamstress mother assume this position a thousand times before, her mouth full of sharp things. So it wasn't the bending, exactly, that made me turn away. It was that I had never seen her do it outside. Never on a chilly Sunday morning in a deserted parking lot at Preston Highway and Outer Loop. I had never seen her be seamstress-supplicant for a white person before, a child at that. The girl and I went to middle school together, and the girl's mother had admired my mother-made dresses. She just had to have some sewn for her own daughter, who had always reminded me, not unpleasantly, of a piglet. But my mother and I lived in Newburg, so there was no question of this lady and her *(pink, soft, round)* daughter braving those wilds to get measured. Neither would my mother be darkening the doorway of this white woman's house in Okolona.

II.

My father's tongue is slow-country Tennessee and my mother's is small-town Kentucky, but I consider my first language to be poetry. My mother brought me home from Louisville Baptist Hospital, to Newburg, to a stanza of my own. That means *room* in English, my second language.

III.

You have such a vivid imagination, teachers at Hartstern Elementary would marvel, before I even knew what that meant. At the time, to me it sounded like a technicolor way of saying I didn't fit in, but I knew that already. I began to spin stories about where I was from. Not Newburg, but Okolona, the majority-white neighborhood to the south. Okolona is where I once visited a paint store with my mother, where I asked if the white paint there could make me into a white girl, a peaches-and-cream precious girl. Years later: I am proud of being Black, of my skin that sings in the sun. I forget about wanting to be someone else. One day out of the blue, my mother asked me, *Remember when you wanted to paint yourself white?* I crumpled inside. I had hoped that I had imagined that.

IV.

My cousins lived in the West End, and they said my brother and I lived in "the country." I couldn't see it at the time. The country? We lived in same Louisville they did. Didn't my father, who started sharecropping at six years old, constantly complain of how close together the houses were in our neighborhood? *I can hardly see the moon anymore*, he said.

Later, I remember: walking to a bus stop with no sign, just a dirt road where the bus drivers knew to stop. Bare field. And beyond, fields of soybean and corn. The last farmhouses almost completely erased by the advance of tract housing. Don't call it suburbia, call it palimpsest: traces of barbed-wire fencing still lined the road.

When I passed through Rangeland Road toward Poplar Level, I always looked left. Stables and ruined cars and rusting farm equipment were tangled in what seemed like a junkyard wonderland to me at the time. If I looked left at just the right moment, I could catch sight of a horse's tail, mid-swing. *Swishhhh*. A scrawl in the wind, a message just for me.

V.

"You don't act like other people I know from Newburg," a fellow student blurted, when I first landed at Berea College. "Not ghetto," she added, as if I needed the translation. In Berea, I'm 114 miles from home and misread here, too.

The streets near my childhood house all start with R, because some developer was ardent about alliteration. I rode my bike down Revere. Ridgecrest Road. Rural Way. That student was right, though—I wasn't ghetto. I was Ratchet.

VI.

A little later, still at Berea, I met another student from Louisville. A white man in his sixties, back in school after years suspended in alcohol. When we get to exchanging neighborhoods, he said, "It's amazing you even made it to college, considering where you came from."

VII.

I'd be lying if I said if I didn't initially receive those slurs as compliments. Didn't I spend years saying I was from Okolona? I tried this with another student at Berea, an older Black woman. When I said I was from Okolona, she asked for streets, receipts. When I handed them over, she was like, "Oh, you're from Newburg then." I stumbled, caught in my lie. I still couldn't come clean, saying, "Oh, I—I thought you wouldn't know where Newburg was." She replied, "Girl, I told you I knew Louisville." She fell quiet, eyeing me. Even now I can still see her eyes narrowing, and inside them, how small I had become.

VIII.

Never mind my neighborhood—I wasn't terribly proud of being from Da Ville, period. As kids we passed around jokes like:

Question: "Why is it called 'Kentuckiana'?"

(Beat.)

Answer: "Because it sounds better than Indiucky!"

The best we could hope for? To steer clear of the "yucky" of the region and be content with being bland and between—neither North nor South, neither banjo Bluegrass nor cosmopolitan city. When I was a teenager, I visited Atlanta with my schoolmates; when we told a local where we were from, he threw back his head and laughed. *Y'all call that a city?*

In French class, Madame told us that kids in Paris learned about Ohio River just as we were learning about the Seine. Ça alors! We couldn't believe it. How could that twist of water muscling its way past downtown matter *in another country?* We had already internalized the notion that the noteworthy and the interesting were perennially elsewhere.

A few years later, I was leaning against the wall of a club on Bardstown Road. The atmosphere was blue smoke and red party lights warring with that haze. I was almost old enough to be holding a drink. The friend I came to the club with introduced me to her friend, a man from Syria. He asked where I was from. "From here," I answered, batting the air as if to push away hometown banality. "But Muhammad Ali is from here," he replied, voice rising. Of course I knew this—after all, my mother had gone roller-skating with him when he was Cassius Clay. "You don't know how much he means to Muslims around the world," he continued. "Being from the same place as Muhammad Ali ... well, that's really special."

I don't remember the name or address of that club, or even the name of the man. What stayed with me: the idea that Louisville could be an almost sacred spot on the world map. To people not born and raised here, at least. I would need more time and travels of my own to alchemize my relationship to my birthplace.

IX.

My mistress' eyes are nothing like the sun. If there was no poetry in where I was from, I would fill my mouth with it. I set myself to memorizing and reciting Shakespeare's sonnets. I walked to my classes in high school, to my after-school job, under the trees, to movies alone: all in iambic pentameter. *If snow be white, why then her breasts are dun.* (My breasts were dun.) I was hoping this exercise would sinew my memory, although there was so much to leave behind in Newburg. Walk/the line, walk/the line. This is where you turn back, repeat, go back to where you came from, until you remember it perfectly. *I grant I never saw a goddess go.*

X.

Pushing forty, I wasn't done lying about where I was from. After years living out of state, I decided to try Louisville again. In particular, I set my sights on finding a spot in the Highlands or in Old Louisville. My sister, who had never left Kentuckiana, joked, "That's you alright. Cats and hardwood floors." I could see it, too: a quiet charm of a place, filled with my books, plants, and of course, purring. Unfortunately, I couldn't find a landlord who shared my vision.

Invariably landlords would ask what neighborhood I grew up in, and "Okolona" was my answer. This time, it wasn't so much shame but the fact of real estate racism. I was unsettled by what I found when I Googled Newburg those days.

Peter1948 on city-data.com wrote:

"...the neighborhood known as 'Newburg' which is south of the Watterson (I-264), is one of the only suburban ghettos in the city and should largely be avoided."

With the subject line, "Proceed with caution," wmac62 chimed in:

"Newburg South of the Watterson is not bad if you like gunfights, you have access to body armor, your rental property includes an underground bunker. You hire a Personal Security Detail to escort in and around your neighborhood. Your rental property includes a security fence with three strands of concertina wire. If you like to smoke or get high I highly recommend this area, other than that I don't see any downside to Newburg."

And on and on, until I couldn't bear to read any more.

I had hoped that obscuring my origins would get me housed, as my savings were being rapidly depleted by my Fern Creek extended-stay hotel room. The truth is, I could say I was from any zip code I wanted—but I was still clearly Black. My cousin shared her own rental woes: even when she and her husband offered to pay six months' rent in advance, they got turned away. I kept looking and calling about places throughout the city and Southern Indiana. Soon after learning that a sweet carriage house in Old Louisville was out of reach, I left for a gig in Washington, D.C., and never returned.

XI.

No sonnet would be complete without the volta, which means "turn" in Italian. It's when the argument in the poem changes key; I loved hunting for this part of the sonnet, as if to unlock it. You put your finger between the octave or sestet, or before the final couplet, and feel the ground of the poem shift.

A few years ago, I took to Googling Newburg once again. This time, I found something different. During all of my growing-up years in Newburg, never had I known its historical heft, its testament to environmental racism. Never had I known that present-day Newburg was once called "Wet Woods," and because of its swampiness, was the only land that freedwoman Eliza Curtis Hundley Tevis was permitted to buy in the 1820s-30s. (Some accounts say the 1850s.) Never had I known that nearby Petersburg, which has since been absorbed into Newburg, had been named after Peter Laws, a freedman who also bought land in the Wet Woods post-Civil War. And that the Petersburg/Newburg Cemetery—Forest Home Cemetery is one of the oldest Black burial grounds in the state.

What other stories do I have yet to unearth about my homeplace?

XII.

That historical heft, humph. I shouldn't need that to counterbalance the weight of carrying Newburg and its stigma. I look askance at my volta. Where I come from is hallowed ground, period. I didn't need old clippings from the *Courier-Journal* or diary entries from slave owners to tell me that. Except ... I did.

Time to stop lying about where I came from. Not just about substituting Okolona for Newburg in my origin stories, but about the caustic shame I came from, am still coming from.

XIII.

Consider the floodplain, how it overwrites it all. Trace your fingers over this shale lowland, and recall. Don't call it poor drainage, call it palimpsest. In writing this it occurs to me that maybe there is a reason why water insinuates itself in almost every nighttime dream of mine. (I mean: snow, shore, lake, mop bucket spill, waterfall, salt pool, isthmus, faucet leak, flooding, frequent flooding.) More than anything else, my memory is marsh, is mud over bedrock.

XIV.

I live downriver now, in Pittsburgh. Without even trying to, I once again followed the thread of water and homeplace. Most of my life thus far has been lived along one waterway above others, the Ohio. Sometimes I joke with my wife about boating down to Louisville from Pittsburgh, instead of driving down via interstate. Sailing down the Ohio River, instead of being sold down the river like my ancestors (as the Mississippi River, the Ohio River, and chattel slavery haunt that idiom).

When out of state, initially I say I am from Kentucky, not Louisville. It's more expedient that way. If I pronounce my hometown as we do, people ask me to repeat myself: "What? What did you say?" That's when I sound out *Louie-ville*, like it's not my mother tongue (it's not). Otherwise, I get good-naturedly teased for speaking in muddle-mutter. But the way Louisvillians murmur *Looavul* is far more poetic and mysterious. Try it. Under this bluegrass, I told you that there is mud. Just put it in your mouth and sing.

Tachean Ho-Tep: Mummy at the Louisville Science Center

KATHLEEN DRISKELL

I.

Excited flurry of bees,
striped in khaki and blue,
they swarm from the school-bus doors
and up the stairs to surround me,
palm-prints on the glass,
nose-smudges on the glass,
they think I am
a goddess,
immortal, and you, teacher,
lingering behind,
your face against the glass, too,
as if it is a church window,
what think
you of me?

2,500 years ago, in my hot kitchen,
a star exploded
in my head.
As I lay there
I smelled bread
burning in my oven.
That aroma still wanders
through my emptied veins.

By the time the miller came home,
he found me dead,
but I was not yet unspooled into the heavens.
I watched from the rafters
as they carried me out,
as the miller gave over all his grain to the priests,
as the embalmers filled me with salt and herbs,

as I was washed with wine,
          as I was left in a dark tomb
in the Valley of the Queens.

          You read there,
                    teacher, on my plaque
I am no Goddess.
          I was no Queen.

          I was a housewife,
middle-class, very
          pretty it was said, but
I was no queen.

And did I ever once lay in the miller's coarse arms
          and sigh for immortality? Besides, it was not for me

               that he gave over all
               to have the priests
               wrap me in linen finery.
                    Into my cold ear, he whispered
                         Talk sweetly to Osiris, bid him
                    when my time comes
                         to let you open heaven's door for me
                         as I had you do here on earth.
          For thirty years, each noon, the Miller shielded
his eyes and looked up, hoping
     to see me traveling
          in the sun's fine painted boat gliding across the sky.

He did not know
     that for centuries I lay in the dark.

          II.
          For two thousand years, I practiced my ritual confession:
          I have done no evil against any man.
          I have not done that which is hated by the gods.
          I am not a worker of wickedness.
Two thousand years, I waited for the door to open,

and when it did, the sun lit
but another pyramid on the stone wall.

III.
Though, finally, I crossed water.
I rocked across the blue for weeks
and when we docked, I thought I'd come heaven's gate.

Again, I practiced my recitation.
I am not a murderer.
I have not snared the birds consecrated to the gods.
I have not taken fish from holy lakes,

but no one asked me to speak,
I was only told to be
still, here, there,
faces and faces leaning in
close, their sour living breath blowing over me.
Why be a god if you are but a thing
to be so coarsely regarded?

IV.

I did float in a river of death, once. You, teacher,
tell the children
how the great floods of 1937
rushed into this city, and how the water rushed
upon this city, and how the water rose against
the marble walls of my gallery, how giant
fishes with the snouts of crocodiles swam all around me,
until I finally spilled out of my stone coffin

and how, though, the waters were rough,
I floated like a thimble, peacefully,
down Liberty, down Broadway, down Market.
Would you believe me if I said
I thought the gods of the dead
had at last summoned me?

V.

Never mind. Do tell the boys how my head
separated from my shoulders—boys like
                    hearing such things—but don't

                    tell the girls how I watched myself float apart,
          so that I could see most clearly
          how I had been overcooked all these years,
      had turned into something that looks
                    moth-eaten, dark like dried fruit.

      I was promised that when I revisited earth, I would be
          a yellow bird,
                    a red-winged beetle,
a blue feather rocking
      gently in the wind.

          They all lied.

VI.

I have not been called because I cannot say:
          I have not caused men to hunger.

          Teacher, how the miller chased my maiden
          skirts around our kitchen, hot hearts
          of household panting together in that dark place,

          my husband's heart was lean
          and stringy. He eyed me as if I were something to eat
          and he was a wild dog on the streets

          Have you, like me, had to make your heart a pillow,
      a place for a man to lay
                    his head after love—all amongst the portent glow
          of the hot kitchen fire,

for if not watched don't the hottest fires
          soon turn to coldest ash?

Like him, you think I might be a goddess?

Is that why you linger? Do you understand that
          to lie next to
                    a man who always wants to enter you, can make
                    any woman want
to close the doors of her own body—still,

     to roll a boulder across the opening
          of a body brings another kind of death.

               VI.
               My head bobbed in the flood's current

like an old jug, but how I traveled!
          I heard the oars cutting the sun-boat's path
          in the water!

     I have not turned aside the water.
     I have not put out the fire when it should burn.
     I have not prevented the temple cattle from grazing on my land.

But the notes of the water music came from an unpainted boat.
          Paddling, two boys, not much older than your students.
                    What's that? one boy said.
I saw a soft white face lean over the edge.
          I don't know. Fish it out, said the other.
Oh, my gosh, they both said, realizing
                    they had brought in not a fish,

but a head! My head rolled, returned into my coffin
          and so it lay in my arms for years until
          I was stitched back together.

Like Frankenstein
a little boy once said
as he was reading my museum note
to his mother.
They turned away, disappointed, they had hoped—
I was something grander than I really was.

But what am I, what was I ever, but a thing
that has been made
and now is condemned
to float forever
in this glass boat of accruing
animal knowledge?

Taking My Toddler to Wilson Pickett's Grave

PATRICK WENSINK

It wasn't until my toddler played King Kong with a metal casket gurney that it hit me: mausoleums are not made for field trips.

I had promised my eighteen-month-old, Walter, we'd be on our way right after paying respects to soul music's most passionate voice and Louisville's most overlooked grave. Following this quick detour we'd check out all the giraffes and apes and bears he could stomach.

You see, Wilson Pickett was buried near the zoo.

This trip was something I planned for over a week, which is a Normandy Invasion-level of forethought in a stay-at-home parent's world. I had decided it was never too early for kids to learn about soul music and elephants. I would knock both out in one morning. Needless to say, the boy whose passion in life involves eating sand was only impressed by one.

Evergreen Cemetery butts against Preston Highway, sandwiched between the airport and Male High School—Hunter S. Thompson's alma mater. The cemetery's massive stretch of land displayed a lot of grey sky thanks to a population of young trees. The gates had just opened for the morning so the only other people on the grounds were gravediggers operating backhoes and trucks.

Pickett's mausoleum stood clustered among a few similar stone buildings at the farthest end of the property. Upon first glance, its stone pillars and lack of windows make the mausoleum look more like a government office building. Slightly more cheerful than the DMV. Unlike the DMV, its single, open room was empty and silent when Walter and I entered. The first thing I noticed was how calming the white marble walls were with all the light flowing in.

Those walls were dotted with brass grave markers, many decorated with flowers and mementos. Pickett's was so subtle it took searching to locate. His plot was along the left-hand wall, couched between similar name plates. Wilson Pickett's final resting place made no mention of his hit records or the thousands of people he thrilled. Not even an apology for appearing in *Blues Brothers 2000*.

There was only an understated bronze bust of the soul pioneer—a youthful, smiling likeness.

WILSON PICKETT, JR
MARCH 18, 1941 – JANUARY 19, 2006
TO OUR BELOVED FATHER, GRANDFATHER, BROTHER, FRIEND AND COMPANION. YOU WERE GREATLY LOVED AND WONDERFULLY APPRECIATED. REST IN PEACE. YOU WILL BE MISSED.

I held my squirming son in my arms and pointed. "This guy right here," I said. "Created soul music. A lot of people will argue, but don't listen. Wilson Pickett put together gospel and R&B and rock and pretty much invented soul music." We admired his tomb another second. "This is important. You need to know this."

Walter let loose a pained yowl that commanded I release him to the wild.

I would have to wait until he was older to explain Pickett's Zelig-like musical career. The man wasn't of a single city or scene like, say, Otis Redding or Smokey Robinson. He was the voice of red dirt southern soul, bouncing around from Stax Studios in Memphis, to Alabama's Muscle Shoals, to American in Memphis.

He left a trail of hit records, including "In the Midnight Hour," "Mustang Sally," and "Land of 1,000 Dances."

"Wicked" Wilson Pickett also left a trail of trouble. He was known to be difficult to work with and had substance-abuse problems. He was obsessed with guns. Pickett was even sentenced to a year in prison after driving drunk and hitting a pedestrian in 1993.

"That's kind of soul music as a whole. Ridiculous highs and awful lows," I said, more to myself than Walter, who had wandered from sight. "That's kind of life as a whole."

Walter remained unimpressed. After only a few minutes he had plucked silk roses from low graves, removed an American flag from another and left a trail of broken crackers across a church pew. Had he been proficient with a lighter, I had no doubt there'd have been a bonfire somewhere.

Wilson Pickett was buried alongside his mother, Lena. Rumor had it Pickett abandoned his childhood home in Alabama to escape her abuse at age fourteen. A move to Detroit, to be near his father, began Wilson's singing career.

Before Lena's death, Wilson was known to frequent Louisville, where she had relocated. It's safe to say the Picketts must have found a way to forgive one another. Aside from buying one of those broken heart "Best Friends" lockets, I can't imagine a stronger sign of forgiveness than choosing to be buried beside someone.

Pickett's grave marker was decorated with a simple white flower and a colorful silk bouquet. Red, yellow, orange, purple. Fiery and alive, like his music. There was a greeting card taped beside it. The cover featured two empty beach chairs and the inscription, "I Miss You."

Inside, in delicate cursive, someone wrote:

LOVE YOU FOREVER.
YOUR OTHER HALF,
GAIL

Gail, I later discovered, was Pickett's fiancée when he died of a heart attack. Gail must have visited recently. She must still be in love.

I closed the card and considered how strong her love must have been. I remained impressed until a thick metallic clang echoed through the mausoleum. Walter had knocked over the aforementioned foldable aluminum gurney. By the time I rushed over, he was joyfully spinning the hard rubber tires. "Come on," I said, setting the gurney back up. "Let's go see the alligators or something."

We headed off to the zoo, and I was disappointed. My aim was to teach Walter about soul music, but he was too busy being a kid. Exiting onto Preston Highway under the overcast sky, I realized maybe I taught him more about soul than I suspected.

Toddlers are in a constant stage of absorption. Walter is always repeating things I don't think he overhears, like curse words and Guy Fieri catchphrases. Here in a single marble room was a great place to absorb the definition of soul music. Wilson Pickett's grave was the intersection of love and death and forgiveness.

Dissect any soul song from Pickett, to Aretha Franklin, to Al Green and you will find at least one of those three elements at its core.

Hopefully, Walter will remember.

Hopefully, he will also remember that gurneys are not toys.

Muhammad Ali's Hometown Heartbreak: I Went Looking for Ali's Louisville, and It Wasn't There

DANA MCMAHAN

When you take an assignment as a freelance writer, you write that story. Never would you pitch an idea, then come back to the editor to tell them you can't do it. Unless, that is, you were trying to write a travel story about the legacy of Muhammad Ali in Louisville in 2014.

My idea, for the travel section of a big newspaper, was a piece that might inspire Ali fans to head to my city of Louisville. The champ was born here in 1942, so it's natural that the millions who revere the man might journey to his hometown. They could see the house where he grew up and follow an Ali trail of sorts through his developing years. It sounded good in the email, and the editor gave me the thumbs up.

I led the nascent story with a line from Ali himself: *Wherever I go I tell 'em I'm from Louisville. I don't want Chicago or New York or Texas to take the credit for all of what I've done. I want you to know … that we in Louisville are the greatest of all time.*

Thunderous applause greeted these words from Muhammad Ali when he spoke them in his hometown in 1978.

Everybody has to come from somewhere, but for Louisvillians, it's an immense source of pride that the champ, the Greatest, Muhammad Ali himself grew up here. That before this living legend shook up the world he was once a kid named Cassius Clay playing in the West End.

The trouble was, I wasn't so sure my words were true. I patched together a limping, scattered story, but couldn't bring myself to file it. Instead, I sent the editor an apology: "After a summer of researching, reading, talking to (many) people, and going all over town, the result is a story that not a single person would read and want to come to Louisville."

See, I'd found that most places significant in Ali's life were unmarked, abandoned, or demolished.

I'd tried. The story encouraged "intrepid" visitors to hunt down Ali's past—going to the park where he ran, touring the building where he had his first job—and included details like how he loved Krispy Kreme on Bardstown Road, but only when the sign is on to say they're fresh.

But what of that would compel anyone to board a plane for Louisville? The city-owned park—which was one of only a few in Louisville open to African Americans until 1955—had no signage to pay homage to the future boxing champion's runs. Would anyone really arrange time with an archivist to see the library where the young man worked (and fell asleep after workouts)? It was a stretch—I was grasping at straws to conjure up a story that didn't exist.

But I just so wanted it to exist— *I* wanted to find Ali's legacy. Like so many, I've found inspiration in his bravery, his relentless pursuit of what is right, his refusal to bow down to anyone. And we humans are driven to find a connection, no matter how fleeting, with those we admire.

Ali himself understood the pull of connecting with a legend. In Thomas Hauser's *Muhammad Ali: His Life and Times* we see Cassius Clay, Sr. take his young son to a tree that boxing great Joe Louis touched. Ali marveled that he could place his own hand on something once touched by the great man. Connecting today with Ali's history and legacy in the city where he laughed and dreamed and fought and played should be as easy as reaching out to touch that tree. But as I scoured our city, the trails I sought lead to dead ends.

Sure, there's the shiny Ali Center. It's excellent, a lovely testament to the man's life. But what about Ali's early years? People travel from around the world and hand over fistfuls of money to tour Graceland in Memphis, to push up against ropes surrounding rooms where Elvis lived. The modest home where Muhammad Ali grew up, meanwhile, was deteriorating. I told a couchsurfer from Slovakia who overnighted at my home that I could show him Ali's old house, and he couldn't believe his luck. On our way to the Greyhound station I drove him by the house. As this twenty-six-year-old who'd grown up a world away—and long after Ali's triumphs—snapped photos, I cringed at the broken-down house.

"Don't bother your head about that house," a brash nineteen-year-old boxer named Cassius Clay told a *Sports Illustrated* reporter in 1961. "One of these days they're liable to make it a national shrine."

On that morning in 2014, though, the dilapidated house stood vacant, only a plaque at the street noting that anything important happened here. It took a team of investors from out of state to right this wrong, and only days before Ali's death did the Muhammad Ali Child-hood Home museum finally open. The champ was right in the end. But was he really, though?

My city celebrates many things well. We love our bourbon and we entice tourists with bourbon trails galore. Our food scene is gaining national recognition, we have a "Hot Brown Hop," and then of course there's that horse race every May. Yes, all of these things are like the other: we're talking about pastimes traditionally enjoyed by white folks of the South with money to spend. But you know what we haven't celebrat-ed—I mean *really* celebrated? (At least not until now that he's gone, after the flowers piled up like the words of city leaders rushing to praise him.) The life of a strong Black man who spoke his mind. Where is our Ali trail? The obligatory, accessible, downtown museum is our one and done.

Ali's hero Joe Louis was beloved in Detroit like our champ was to many of us. I thought Louis' hometown legacy was headed the same way as Ali's when his longtime training center, the Brewster Wheeler building, was slat-ed for demolition. Then, enter Kid Rock. The musician had a friend who wanted to open a restaurant at the site and preserve the building. In a city where getting streetlights is a challenge and dangerous abandoned struc-tures are razed daily, they saved the building. "When this redevelopment is completed, we will have a facility that honors the legacy of Joe Louis, Leon Wheeler and so many others, and re-establishes its connection to the com-munity," mayor Mike Duggan said. (Wheeler was the city's first African American recreation worker.) "It's important that we remember our history and we celebrate it."

There was no such celebrity fanfare to keep a similar monument to Ali's early training, the Presbyterian Community Center (formerly known as the Grace Hope Community Center), open to the community when the Smoketown neighborhood institution closed in 2013. A historian might be able to point out the location, but its significance wouldn't be clear to the casual visitor. (The public school system now owns the building, where it operates an early childhood education program.)

Could it be because we're ashamed? We should be. After the Olympic champion returned home from taking the 1960 gold he was turned away from a restaurant. We may never know if the legend of Ali tossing his medal in the Ohio River after that humiliation is true, but if he did it, who can blame him? More local lore has it that a prestigious private club, the kind patronized by wealthy civic leaders, refused for years to change the address on their letterhead after the street was renamed for Muhammad Ali. I'd make like Ali and leave town, too. Because, of course, it's not just Ali's legacy that isn't tangible in Louisville. Ali himself moved away long ago.

Now that he's gone for good, we're honoring Ali, loudly and publicly. And for many it is sincere. But why does it come when he's a memory, not a man? Why bring flowers to his home now, but not care when weeds were growing up in front of the house he thought would be a shrine?

Louisville had a hard time knowing how to deal with Muhammad Ali, this peace-loving fighter, a proud Muslim who dared to tell the world he was the greatest, who defied expectations of the time when he refused to take up arms against a people he had no quarrel with. "Why should they ask me to put on a uniform and go 10,000 miles from home and drop bombs and bullets on Brown people in Vietnam while so-called Negro people in Louisville are treated like dogs and denied simple human rights?" he famously asked. Many in Louisville could never forgive that.

We may like to think now the time is gone that someone would be turned away for the color of their skin, but we now have a president who turns them away from our borders. Louisville is but a reflection of the world that was and that is, a world that is uneasy with power in those that are *other*.

After Ali's death, all eyes turned to Louisville and once again I wished I could try writing that travel story. Not with a trail of artifacts to follow, but with Ali's living legacy, that of a city where many strive—more quietly than Ali, but with no less dedication—for love and equality. A place dubbed a compassionate city, where we hold a Festival of Faiths (with the organizer's office on Muhammad Ali Blvd!), where a pay-it-forward restaurant opened not far from where Ali grew up.

But would that story have been any better than the first one I pitched? Sure, parks are no longer segregated, but our city as a whole remains starkly divided by race and income. Where can I show a true effort by city leaders to remove barriers to opportunity for all when we've yet to elect a Black or female mayor? As I grieve for this man I never met, I mourn, too, for the city he wanted us to be.

Ali gave our undeserving city a gift: testimony to what we can find within ourselves. We didn't do it in his lifetime, but it's not too late to become more than the city of his birth, more than the city that shunned a hero. We can honor his memory beyond words and flowers. We can commit to continue his work. We can earn the right to call ourselves the home of the Greatest.

"The best way to make your dreams come true is to wake up," Ali said. The city of Louisville has rolled out a website that's a start at recognizing the (remaining) sites important to Ali's legacy. Ali's Louisville, "devoted to all things Ali in his hometown," collects several of the touchpoints I sought for that first, failed travel story.

Change happens slowly, but it's happening. After Ali's death in 2016, Spalding University honored him by hanging a red bicycle—a replica of that famous stolen red Schwinn that motivated a young Cassius Clay to learn how to fight—over the front door of its athletics building at 824 South Fourth Street. In 2018, on what would have been Ali's 76th birthday, Spalding changed the name of the building to Columbia Gym, in honor of the training facility run out of its basement by Louisville police officer Joe Martin, the man who first taught Ali how to box there. Two years later, a historical marker was dedicated, telling anyone who passed by that history had been made at that spot.

And then in 2019, the city took a huge step forward in celebrating Ali as a hometown hero by renaming the airport after him. Now anyone who flies into Louisville will know upon landing whose city they're in. It's just too bad it took a funeral to get us here. I hope it's only the beginning of what we do in Ali's memory.

Ali faced the worst in people and gave them back the best. No matter how profound the cost, he stood fast to his beliefs—that all deserve respect and love. He wasn't showered with love in his city, yet he showered unending love on humanity. And his truest legacy won't actually be found in buildings or historical markers, but in the mark he made on our hearts—in Louisville and around the world.

Cave Hill Cemetery, Louisville, KY

NANCY MCCABE

A tarnished St. Francis releases a dove.
An actual robin hops across the stone
of a pet bird named Pretty Polly.
Geese loiter in the road,
sparrows dip through dogwoods.
They will soar on wings of eagles,
says the Kessler family stone.

And I'm jealous: my dad,
in an austere Kansas cemetery,
beneath an economical upright marker,
along rows of stones like plump pillows
has no birds to bridge the gap
between heaven and earth,
no messenger pigeon to carry news
to the afterlife, though he
loved birds as much as

George Keats, brother of John, or
the writers of the Happy Birthday Song,
or the composer of a Confederate tune
called "Think of Your Head in the Morning"
or the magician whose caped sculpture plays
one last, eternal trick, hollow eyes
catching the sun and glittering creepily.

They get a graveyard full of birds:
bronze, granite, limestone, hollow bones, keratin,
flocking upward in an etching
for a young baseball player, gathering
around a miniature birdbath for a child
who rode her trike into the family pool.

But never mind, Dad: here is another
father who should have had a bird,
but doesn't. There's no marble chicken
on Colonel Sanders' grave.
Instead, his daughter carved a poem about
how she's like a dancer hovering above the earth
as "God plucks the chords of the harp."
Pluck seems an appropriate verb.

I don't even get a poem in granite,
just this one, scrawled on notebook paper,
my message to the afterlife,
to a dad who overcooked our chicken,
whose musty backyard pigeons I disdained,
battering each other in frenzies of wings,
chattering like old men clearing their throats.
I remember the times we fought, battering
each other with frenzies of words

but that time a sparrow flew down my chimney
you plucked it right out of the air,
calm magician, and then, fierce pitcher
tossed it out the door. It hovered there, dazed,
before its wings took over where your hands left off,
before it rose into its own memory of flight.

A Peculiar Composition

MICHAEL L. JONES

Cave Hill Cemetery is where Louisville, Kentucky, buries its legends. Its 296 acres are dotted with monuments and historical markers honoring notable figures. Among them are George Rogers Clark, the Revolutionary War general who settled Louisville in the 1770s; former heavyweight boxing champion Muhammad Ali, known early in his career as the "Louisville Lip"; and Colonel Harland Sanders, who gave the world Kentucky Fried Chicken. But there are no historical markers in Cave Hill for Mildred Jane Hill and Patty Smith Hill, the sisters responsible for the most popular song in the English language—"Happy Birthday to You." Mildred and Patty, born in 1859 and 1868, are interred in a small family plot with headstones bearing only their names and the year each was born and died.

Growing up in Louisville, I was taught that "Happy Birthday" was written by two local white kindergarten teachers—that's it. But then I learned more about the Hill sisters' unlikely story in the early nineties, when I was researching my book about Louisville jug band music, and in 2011, when my wife and I bought a house one street away from Kenwood Hill Road, where the sisters had a summer cabin. My wife is the president of the Little Loomhouse, the nonprofit that currently owns the property. The Hill sisters' cabin fell down decades ago due to neglect, but three other similar board-and-batten cabins—called Esta, Tophouse, and Wisteria— are still there. I've sung "Happy Birthday" at parties in Esta, where local legend says the song was performed for the first time.

Today, when the Hill sisters are remembered by name, the focus is usually on Patty, a nationally renowned pioneer in early childhood education. Patty lived until 1946, long enough to see the success of the song she wrote with her sister. But Mildred has always interested me more. In addition to being a composer, she was an early ethnomusicologist, documenting the African-American music that permeated the streets, riverboats, and churches of Louisville in the late 1800s. She also incorporated these sounds into her most famous composition.

I discovered the connection between "Happy Birthday" and Black music after reading "History of Music in Louisville," a piece Mildred wrote for a book commemorating Louisville's first one hundred years. In it, she wrote, "If a history of music in Kentucky were being written, a large portion should be devoted to the music of the Negro in our State . . . The old Negroes, who alone know this music, are fast dying out, and it is sad that some effort is not made to secure it before it is too late."

Mildred did all she could to preserve this music. In 1898, the Louisville Commercial reported, "Miss Hill is an authority on this subject, having given much time to the collection of old Negro songs, which if not collected and preserved will soon be lost to us forever." It was unusual for a woman of Mildred's status to be championing Black culture in nineteenth-century Louisville. After the Civil War, the city was a magnet for ex-Confederates because it was the headquarters of the Louisville & Nashville Railroad, which controlled all the intact Southern rail lines to the Deep South, and was a major hub for riverboat traffic to New Orleans. The ex-Confederates took control of Louisville's social, business, and political life. In doing so, they instituted some Southern norms which had not previously existed in Louisville. After the war, most entertainment and social interactions became segregated. This was the atmosphere during the time Mildred was spending her Sundays in African American churches transcribing spirituals.

Mildred was raised to be a free thinker. Her father, the Reverend William Wallace Hill, was criticized for allowing the teaching of geology at the Bellewood Female Seminary, a girls' school he founded in Anchorage, Kentucky, just outside of Louisville. Mildred began her musical training at Bellewood. Shaken by the memory of widows left destitute after the war, Rev. Hill treated his four daughters and two sons equally, encouraging them all to develop careers. After his death, when Mildred was nineteen, the Hill sisters were determined to find work to support the family and put their two brothers through college.

Patty became principal of a demonstration kindergarten at the Louisville Free Kindergarten Association. She found the songs being used in class to be of poor quality and too hard for the children to sing. Between 1889 and 1893, she and Mildred collaborated on a number of songs more appropriate for the classroom. The Hill sisters used the street cries of Black vendors for inspiration. These vendors usually had one line that they would repeat with variations. Patty's lyrics were short and repetitive, making them easy for children to remember after hearing them only once or twice. Likewise, Mildred's melodies were simple enough for small children to sing. In an 1895 letter, Mildred wrote, "I collected [the street cries] just for the interest I took in them never expecting to make any use of them but since I began the study of composition I have found them very useful."

One of the first tunes the Hill sisters wrote was called "Good Morning to All":

Good Morning to You
Good Morning to You
Good Morning, dear children
Good Morning to All!

Although their compositions seem simple, the songs were developed through an exacting process. After a song was written, Patty—sometimes accompanied by Mildred—taught it to her class. If the students had trouble with any part of it, the sisters would revise the song and then present a new version. After they had a final version, Patty would sometimes write new verses to the melody for other occasions. "Good Morning to All" became "Good-bye to You," "Happy Journey to You," "Happy Christmas to You," and "Happy Birthday to You."

The recent discovery of Mildred Hill's notebooks and compositions in the holdings of the Dwight Anderson Memorial Music Library at the University of Louisville confirms the influence of African-American music on the development of the famous song. "It is very clear that she was interested in all types of folk music, but particularly slave songs, hymns, and street cries," said library director James Porcell. "There is a sort of scrapbook where she clipped and pasted all sorts of articles related to them, including her own."

The Hill sisters' publications and speeches on African-American music reveal that they accepted some racist concepts that were originally used to justify the institution of slavery and continued to be popular in educated circles in the decades following Emancipation. Chief among them was the cultural theory that African Americans were considered to be in a primitive state equivalent to a child in civilized society. This is one reason the Hill sisters thought Black music would connect with young students. In an 1895 article concerning her field work on African-American street cries, Mildred wrote, "After all, for the negro is like a child, in that his tears and mirth follow each other so closely that it is difficult to keep pace with his moods." She continued, "Evade it as we may, the fact remains that the genuine negro music is the most characteristic we have in this country." Thus was the irony of the Hill sisters: they perpetuated ideas about racial inferiority while also recognizing the importance of Black music to the future of American culture.

In 1892, Mildred wrote an article titled "Negro Music" for *Music*, a Chicago journal. She used the pseudonym Johann Tonsor because she was worried that her ideas wouldn't be taken seriously if readers knew she was a woman. Two decades before the appearance of jazz, she claimed that the African-American sound would be the basis of American music in the next century. Mildred, who died in 1916, had no idea that one of her own African-American-influenced tunes would become an enduring part of popular culture.

In 1934, Patty Smith Hill attended a matinee performance of *As Thousands Cheer*, a musical revue by playwright Moss Hart and composer Irving Berlin. By then, she was in her mid-sixties and a professor at Columbia University's Teachers College. During a scene depicting a birthday celebration for John D. Rockefeller, Hill watched in dismay as the cast sang "Happy Birthday to You." The use of the song in a commercial environment shocked her. "I don't think I ever heard it sung myself except when I heard it sung in *As Thousands Cheer*," she said in a deposition for a lawsuit against producer Sam Harris. "I would read in the newspaper that on President Roosevelt's birthday it was sung, and I know that it has been sung at dinners for adults, but I never heard it personally sung that I can remember for anything except educational conferences."

The Harris case was the first of a series of lawsuits that established the Hill family's stake in the ownership of the lyrics and the melody of the song. In 2016, U.S. District Judge George King ruled that "Happy Birthday to You" is now in the public domain based on the 1893 copyright for "Good Morning to All." The decision reminded the public that "Happy Birthday," one of the few songs that is still orally transmitted, is not in fact a folksong. It was written by two women from Kentucky, and now we also know that it was influenced by Black culture. (ASCAP, or the American Society of Composers, Authors and Publishers, has called "Happy Birthday to You" the most popular song of the twentieth century.)

In a 2015 lecture on Mildred Hill, New York University professor Michael Beckerman said, "There is some sense that people probably have that 'Happy Birthday' is a white song or a product of white America. . . . I believe certainly now that the world's most popular song has deep Black roots, deep Louisville roots reflecting Mildred Hill's lifetime commitment to African-American sound, which she believed . . . should be the future."

The Sanctified Present: Louisville Punk, 1978-1982

TIM HARRIS, TARA KEY, AND CHIP NOLD

Louisville, Kentucky, punk rock in the late '70s and '80s was noteworthy for producing a clutch of original bands, each of them distinct from the other, in one of the less likely locations for a fertile scene. Bands like No Fun, the I-Holes, the Endtables, the Blinders, Malignant Growth, the Dickbrains, Strict-9, Your Food, and the Skull of Glee had to pull together the infrastructure in which their bands could rehearse, gig, and maybe record out of the equivalent of rocks, twigs, and a few scraps of leather.

In later years, Louisville artists such as Squirrel Bait, Slint, Rodan, Crain, Will Oldham, and Tara Jane O'Neil would take the stage in a world that had the benefit of college radio, independent record labels, and a club circuit which would book alternative music.

But in 1978 there was only the Word. People in Louisville interested in the music coming out of New York and London began to meet each other, showing up at local record stores or the rare Patti Smith or Elvis Costello show, and ended up creating something all our own. The early scene was not covered on the radio and rarely in the print press, and not booked in the bars and clubs of the era. The book *White Glove Test* (Drag City) documents how the only way to communicate this movement in the pre-digital era were posters, usually stapled to telephone poles.

The first gigs were cataclysmic events filled with excitement. They were one-offs, where somebody agreed to host us for the first and last time. Venues included art galleries, barns, a women's prison, a teenage pregnancy school, a former strip bar, a living room, a basement, a bar in a rough part of town with the sign "No guns allowed inside," a German beer hall, an art school, the St. Matthews Potato Festival, a movie theater, a public library—any available harbor before this music was eventually welcomed into the club scene.

After this initial phase, we started to connect with similar scenes in Lexington, Nashville, Cincinnati, Bloomington, and Lawrence, Kansas.

Members of one of the scene's linchpin groups, the Babylon Dance Band, have been working on a group memoir of their experience, and about the larger community that grew with and around them. What follows are excerpts from that unpublished work, augmented with a few excerpts from elsewhere, that use one band's experience to stand in for the whole scrimping-by, opinionated, raucous group of people who made an imaginative leap into something new.

Tim Harris, bass: The first stirrings of punk rock in Louisville happened when the I-Holes and No Fun cranked up the volume outside of Louisville in Anchorage, at the Louisville School of Art, an institution set on a secluded knoll where the noise could dissipate down the hill and across a stream into the woods.

Tara Key, guitar: When I joined No Fun, I felt like I'd joined my platoon. I really felt that we were going out into the community as an army unit, defending the honor of creativity and expressiveness.

In our little personal drama in 1978 America, it felt like going to battle. There was this sense that we were spreading an epistle, gearing up and armed, and that's the reason that I would often wear … an army helmet when I played.

We began as painters together at LSA, listening to our shared collection of the first blast of punk records: Patti Smith, Blondie, the Ramones, Richard Hell and the Voidoids, Wire, burning through afternoons and evenings together, wordlessly absorbing the sonics while we worked. This led to Bruce Witsiepe and Tony Pinotti spearheading a DIY response with Skip Koeberman, a teacher, and Dean Thomas, our drummer who, within the year, landed with the rockabilly group Levi and the Rockats.

I was asked to join in and showed up in a crisp white shirt and a tie, the Patti-influenced equivalent of reporting for duty at NASA the first night. I left the sculpture building where we practiced with blood on my shirt from a joyous mauling of an electric guitar, for the first time in unity and communion with other players. It marked the beginning of the rest of my life. I'm not sure I would have ever left my bedroom (where I had spent three or so years writing weepy folk songs that only my cat was witness to) if the agitator boys in No Fun hadn't shoved me off a cliff.

On Derby Day, May 6, we played our first show. We had made the first punk rock in Kentucky.

Chip Nold, lead singer: The first version of the Dance Band was composed of me, my high school friends Tim and Marc, and my friend Laura Lehmann—a talented bluegrass fiddler who knew next to nothing about rock—filling in on drums. Our first gig was in a punk festival held in a Southern Indiana barn—bottom of a bill with No Fun and the I-Holes. The bands set up in one loft. Half the crowd was eight feet down, on the pressed-dirt-and-straw floor; the other half was on the wide loft opposite us. Weird gulfs to play across, but we couldn't be picky about the venue first time out.

Tara: No Fun played this festival as well, and on that day, July 7, 1978, I met my future mate Tim Harris for the first time, sitting on a fence outside the barn. I also saw the Babylon Dance Band for the first time, and felt a little jealous that they were playing covers of the songs I had fallen in love with via an ever-present transistor radio as a kid—the pre-teen fodder of the Monkees and Paul Revere and the Raiders, the songs I had sung into my bedpost/microphone before I had a clue that I could be a performer.

Nedelkoff's barn was a primal location for the Louisville music scene. And Robert Nedelkoff was a prime motivator of our scene; in the case of the Babylon Dance Band, he convinced them that they had a band before they had a band! He was a people connector, making a jigsaw puzzle out of all our disparate pieces.

The barn was in rural Indiana, an aerie perched atop the Knobs that loomed over the Ohio River across from the West End of Louisville. This festival brought together, for the first time, all of the freaks that had been eyeing each other over the previous few months: at the Patti concert or the Rock Class taught at the Highlands branch of the Louisville Free Public Library; the Bowie fans, the *Rock Scene* readers, the cultural misfits fed up with a diet of '70s ennui and musical pablum doled out by the airwaves of Louisville at the time. We knew about the bands on the New York and London scenes. But something in the Ohio River water gave us the gumption to take matters into our own hands, and over the ensuing months after No Fun's debut, a couple of score of us—who had never, prior to this time, entertained the notion of picking up a guitar in public or belting out an original song—did so in short order.

What followed was a cataclysmic four months culminating in No Fun's last gig at the Vogue Theater on August 12, where we took the gospel to the unconverted masses who were in attendance at the Midnight Movie showing of *Fritz the Cat*.

It was prototypical art-as-collision: we broke glass, dodged projectiles, and played only half of our planned set as a mini-rock and roll riot broke out. But also peppered among the crowd were the veterans of the summer season and the next group of intrigued converts.

Then we broke up and the band minus me moved to New York to form Circle X. But puzzlemaster Nedelkoff got me a new gig, suggesting to Chip that he call me up and ask me to join the Dance Band.

Marc Zakem, guitar: What's most instructive about these early days is the critical mass of creativity that was attained within the band. Before and after my time in the band, I couldn't write a song to save my soul, and I wouldn't be able to play most of those songs now. During that time in the band I could also sound some covers out by ear. Since then, zilch.

Chip: As if the situation called forth the superpowers the circumstances required.

Marc: In Louisville, performer and audience were really one and the same (we regularly danced to whomever was on before we took the stage; sooner or later, everyone who had come to see us had his or her own band).

Tim: While all of us in the scene certainly had goals and visions of the future, we were really living in the present tense. Waking up on a Louisville morning in 1978 found us thinking about the next song to write, the next rehearsal, the next gig. Paris in the Twenties, Berkeley '65 or Mexico City 1968!

Chip: So why did we put ourselves in such a weird, lonely position? Why didn't we just head off to New York or wherever people like us were supposed to go?

We weren't masochists. We thought we were evangelists. People needed to hear our music; they needed this loud blast to knock them out of their late-

'70s ruts. You would see conversions in those days—some longhair would hear one of the early Louisville punk bands and show up the next day with visible ears.

Actually, in those days I felt less like a minister, and more like a mathematician waiting for a top journal to publish the proof for his theorem: This is right, and soon enough you'll all realize it.

If you hadn't been converted to punk, however, you might not understand how dramatically an aggregation like ours stood apart from the ordinary run of bands.

From time to time, someone would think we were just another group. We once got booked at the eighth-grade graduation dance of a parochial school. (We had so few opportunities to play for people—to proselytize for our sound—that we would never turn down a show.) What we tore through in our hastily cut-short set was something neither the parents nor any but the wildest kids wanted.

"Don't you know any *Billy Joel*?" one of the moms asked us in an aggressive plaint. "We're very limited people," I deadpanned back.

Punk was a great music for limited people to play. Fucking fast is an easier tempo to play than *andante* or *legato*; the two or three chords most songs require are within the capacities of an amateur guitarist; anger and frustration are emotions within the range of a singer running out of breath from shouting over electric clamor. It might take some getting used to. But if your ears worked the right way, there was nothing more thrilling. Maybe it actually forced you to participate in the art form, the way old-time radio forced you to imagine unseen settings, faces and expressions. We found a Northwest Passage through our limitations by focusing on everyone's strengths.

The first drummer who stuck around for more than a couple of gigs was Dave Bradley. Five years older than the rest of us and a veteran of '60s bands, Dave was a fairly skilled player by the standards of Louisville punk. He brought dynamics—cymbal crashes, drum fills—into songs that might otherwise just have bam-a-lama-ed straight ahead. Our next drummer, Sean Mulhall, was seven years younger than Tim and me, twelve younger than Dave. He made an already loud and fast band louder and faster—but never too hurried that we didn't pack a wallop.

Tim: The first requirement for a rehearsal space is that you don't bother anyone with the noise—specifically, the WHAP! of the snare drum. In the course of the Babylon Dance Band, we practiced in an apartment, a barn, a garage, a basement, a loft at the top of a historic cast-iron building, a parish cafeteria, a tiny suburban office—most of them locales embedded in the interstices of the community, in some sort of Edge City situated either in space (a house bordered by an alley and a fast-food emporium) or in time (setting up the equipment when the office workers have retreated to the suburbs for the night).

But we moved from that office to return to the sort of institution that really makes a scene happen: the rock 'n' roll house.

The punk house at 1069 Bardstown Road was a camelback, with a low exposed outdoor porch where punks would loll on warm evenings, looking across an asphalt parking lot at Arby's. (Between songs, we would repeatedly hear the loudspeaker offering, "Would you like potato cakes with that?")

Chip: The second-floor practice room was up a rickety fire escape that let you feel the full weight of every amp, the ungainliness of every piece of the drum kit. It was scary when it iced over. We had to close the windows when we played, even in the most stiflingly humid Louisville summers. (At one point, mattresses and box springs were nailed up as makeshift sound baffles.) Practices ran from afternoon to nearly midnight.

Tim: At first, the Blinders, BDB, and Dickbrains split the time; then we were joined by Strict-9, who came after high school was out for an afternoon rehearsal. Later, Orange Orange, which begat Your Food, was part of the lineup, and later Circle X.

The bands shared a work ethic, spurred by an underlying competitiveness. We basically practiced seven days or nights a week. All the bands were writing lots of material and looking to the future, or living in some kind of sanctified present.

Chip: 1069 wasn't just a rehearsal space—it was a magnet, a place people could go to "sign up" for the scene. (A few seemed to treat it like a job interview, or fraternity rush.)

Tara: 1069 became, not by design as much as serendipity, our headquarters. It seemed that during most waking hours (and, probably to the dismay of whoever was on the lease at the moment, during non-waking hours as well) there would be one or three or eight of us on the porch, in the living room, in conversation heady, raucous, or silly. Or sitting silently together watching traffic. Or playing four square in the Arby's parking lot. It was our switchboard and touchstone.

Tim: It's certainly amazing that the police never made us shut down 1069.

One time we returned from a gig to unload our equipment in the middle of the night. We pulled our van into the Arby's parking lot and were suddenly surrounded by several police cars with lights flashing; a number of officers piled out to surround us.

What was my reaction? I thanked them. I explained that we were glad they were checking up on this sort of thing because we had concerns about the safety of our amplifiers and instruments and we were glad they were preventing our getting cleaned out in the middle of the night. This wasn't self-conscious bravado—I was serious. I don't remember anything particular about their reaction except that they said something like, "OK, fine, carry on."

I can only hope other members of alternative communities can have the same kind of relationship and get the same kind of treatment from their local police officers.

There would often be people there to watch us rehearse, making every rehearsal sort of like a gig because you wanted to perform well when people were listening. And people seemed really excited to be there. There weren't that many places to have punk rock gigs.

Tara: For a shy girl like me the idea that, over the course of four years, I picked up a guitar and played gigs in these spots was mind-blowing: standing behind a stripper pole at Willo's Tavern; in a bar in Portland, the Schooner, where we acknowledged local custom by playing a stop-and-start version of "Eve of Destruction" to accompany a mop dance. (Whoever got stuck holding the mop was out.)

There was a biker bar turned punk rock haven (the Iroquois Hideaway, later the South 40) in the South End where an attendee rode his Harley through the front door onto the dance floor, and Chip replaced him to sing "City of the Savage Agnostics" from the chopper's seat; the hippie bar I walked by almost every day in my neighborhood (the Headrest); a school assembly of third-trimester pregnant teenagers; and a literally captive audience at a women's prison in Pewee Valley.

In these early years it seemed each gig was either a confrontation, in the worst scenarios, or a cultural experiment, in the best. Eventually, especially after the Hideaway/South 40 accepted us, we found a series of more stable labs where people came to us.

Chip: We also played some gigs down the block from 1069, at Tewligan's Tavern, a former hippie bar (the Funktion Junktion) with a carpet so smoky, sodden, and grungy it's passed into legend.

Chip: In 1979, the Endtables and the O'Bannon brothers' Blinders established themselves on the scene. In 1980, younger bands joined in—the Dickbrains and Malignant Growth.

Tara: There seemed to be a generational shift—now younger folks that had listened to the first group of bands were inspired to do something themselves. That's the lifeblood of a scene—it was a real strengthening of what was going on. Because now you had sympathetic ears that were becoming sympathetic hands and voices.

And it was just an affirmation: "Yes! We're on the right track."

Tim: Gender is an interesting topic in our scene. We thought about it in certain music stores, when condescending rocker guys assumed I was buying a guitar instead of Tara. But mostly we didn't think about it very much. We had women breaking the rules of seventies stereotypes of acoustic folkies by playing lead guitar, bass, and drums. Tina Weymouth was my bass idol as much as Paul Simonon. There was no white-boy hardcore scene yet and no Riot Grrrl scene yet. Steve "Chile" Rigot, the lead singer of the

Endtables, would now be called trans. To us, he was a rock star. The essence of our scene was to enable anyone to be something new.

Tara: In the '60s I bought *16 Magazine*, I bought *Tiger Beat,* and I had pinups on my wall. But it wasn't really like I was fawning over Peter Tork and the Monkees or Mark Lindsay and the Raiders. I didn't really want to go out with them. It's like I always wanted to *be* them. Honestly, it never occurred to me that I couldn't, being a girl. It was always a little bit different here. I think that there were so many women on the scene who were obviously equals to men from the get-go that it just wasn't an issue for me. All my life I've had to acknowledge that it was an issue for other women— but not in 1978 Louisville. It seemed like we did by becoming, not with a demand to be treated equally. We just were.

Chip: One advantage of our lonely position as Louisville punks was that the folks attracted into our scene were, almost by definition, interesting people. At any particular gig, you might find dental students, garbage tippers, professors' kids, drag queens, hellions, salesmen, revolutionary communists, bikers. It was a community that reached across differences of class, musical ability and taste, personality, and sexuality, to make something that had no reason to be, but now seems inevitable. It really wasn't, though, and that's the magic of it.

Brett Ralph of Malignant Growth told me not long ago that he'd watched a documentary on another city's legendary punk scene and found himself astounded that the participants seemed like such pallid personalities. "Where's the Steve Rigot?" he yelled. "Where's the Chris Abromavage? Where's the Tara Key?"

Tim: If you were from somewhere else and didn't know better, you might have assumed this scene was a barren desert of hayseed anti-intellectualism. You would have been sooooo wrong.

Beck Folkerth who sang for the Mindpods went on to teach at Harvard Medical School. Alec Irwin, bass player for the Dickbrains, got multiple graduate degrees and worked for the World Health Organization. Brett Ralph, the second singer for Malignant Growth, had gone to college on a scholarship as an All-County football player, and then became a poet and a college professor.

But I'm not really thinking of later academic and professional achievements, so much as the kind of on-the-scene, day-to-day rigor of those hours between band rehearsals at the punk house. Chip, a Princeton man no less, found himself alone as the only one in a roomful of Louisville punks who had NOT read Stendhal's *The Charterhouse of Parma*.

Chip: Tim is too modest to mention the Phi Beta Kappa key he earned at Indiana University. But Louisville punk was not just a bunch of artists and intellectuals.

Tim: In 1978, during the soundcheck for the Babylon Dance Band's second gig, at the Eclectic Gallery at Second and Main in Louisville, I heard a voice shout for the first time a line that would go down in band history: "Sacrifice the bass!"

Kenny Ogle yelled that phrase in his Kentucky twang, with such friendliness and enthusiasm, that it really became a thing for me: Every time we played, I set out to sacrifice my bass guitar to the punk rock gods.

Often this resulted in bleeding fingers. Sometimes in broken bass strings, and those aren't easy to break. And after some months of playing our rapid-fire assaults, my hard plastic pick had dug an inch-deep hole in the wood surface of my Gibson bass. In some sense, I was doing it for Kenny.

Tara: We used to coat our fingers in Nu-Skin. Because we would literally wear away our cuticles to bloody pulps after doing what we did for four hours a night.

Chip: I didn't yet understand the concept of dehydration. So when we'd play four sets at the South 40, I'd sometimes have to ask the band to play an instrumental so I could run offstage to throw up.

Tim: Kenny and his friend, Mark Abromavage, became de facto roadies for our band for the next year, helping heft the equipment in exchange for free drinks, before they started their own band.

They were inseparable in those years, but they couldn't have been more different. Kenny was always talking, always hatching a scheme. Mark rarely said a word. Kenny had long hair and a sporadic beard. With his flashing eyes, he looked like a portrait of Jesus in a Scandinavian church. Mark had long hair, too, almost halfway down his back, but he was impassive. He just sat there and listened, soaking up everything around him.

They both grew up in the shadow of Louisville's Rubbertown, Louisville's chemical-industrial complex. I somehow felt that those two were genetically transformed from overexposure to dangerous chemicals in their youth, such that they were superior beings, capable of feats of endurance out of the reach of other mortals.

They formed a band called Malignant Growth with Mark's brother Chris on bass, and a fine drummer, Todd Fuller, who went by the name of Sid. Kenny, of course, was the singer. After Kenny left town for the wildcatting fields of Oklahoma, fifteen-year-old Brett Ralph joined up as the singer; they later changed the name to Fadin' Out. Mark later became the lead guitarist in Kinghorse, one of Louisville's biggest bands of the late '80s.

Chip: Most of the bands mentioned here had broken up by 1984 or so (although the Growth soldiered on for a few more years). All of them have songs on the excellent collection *Bold Beginnings: An Incomplete Collection of Louisville Punk 1978-1983* (Noise Pollution, 2007). The Babylon Dance Band reconvened after a decade and released an album, *Four on One*, on Matador Records in 1994. Drag City released an Endtables CD in 2013 and re-released *Poke It With a Stick*, the 1983 album by Your Food—a superb combo that teamed Dickbrains Doug Maxson and Charles Schultz with John Bailey and Wolf Knapp—in 2019.

The Louisville Underground Music Archive at the University of Louisville (library.louisville.edu/archives/luma) is doing a scrupulous job documenting this and many other local music scenes. Wink O'Bannon of the Blinders has put an amazing assortment of Louisville music up on his YouTube channel, hammerofthedogs.

Tim and Tara have had their band Antietam since moving east in 1983; Wolf and Charles played in versions of the group. I sang in the Bulls with John, Charles, and Wink.

The many noteworthy bands that have emerged out of this scene include Languid and Flaccid, the Happy Cadavers (proto-David Grubbs), Squirrel Bait, Maurice, Poor Girls, the Monsters (Rigot and Stephen Jan Humphries from the Endtables, Sandy Campbell of the Blinders, and Ricky Feather), Falconetti (with Bruce Witsiepe of No Fun), Mr. Big (with Sean from the BDB), Bodeco (with Ricky and Wink), Freakwater (with Catherine Irwin of the Dickbrains and Janet Beveridge Bean of the Skull of Glee, and later, Eleventh Dream Day), and Slint, Rodan, and beyond.

Wink and Chile Rigot of the Endtables were in a whole slew of bands together, from the Skull of Glee to the Women Who Love Candy. Wink was in another slew of bands with his brother Michael and Michael's wife, Tari O'Bannon, who sang in the Dickbrains and currently fronts the incredible Juanita, which keeps the spirit of this scene burning bright.

One remarkable thing about the scene is its persistence as a social network. Charles Schultz, who has lived in Manhattan for over thirty years, told me not long ago that when he comes to Louisville he still feels connected to everybody in much the same way as before: "Like cousins," he said.

Punk Rock

BRETT EUGENE RALPH

The nights were blunt and fixed.
Nobody meant anything by anything.
We were fast enough, sure,
But we were kids: we did
Cheap drugs alone and hoped
We wouldn't crumble if somebody fucked us.

Tell City

BRETT EUGENE RALPH

One of them had put on painter's overalls
& bought a bunch of flowers

The flowers got him into
A hospital room

He wasn't under anyone's care
But he had his reasons for being there

What became of them
There's no telling

Dirty yellow ones—the kind
You see everywhere

                *

That was back in the days before
He even knew my name

I never thought he'd know my name
Never thought I'd sit still

To hear such a story
Long light fighting through

The twisted down blinds
Slashes across my face & hands

                *

I thought I would never escape
That room

I never dreamed what I heard there
Would dog me

Never thought I'd see her again
I never thought her mother

Would ask me for money
Give it to me, she whispered

Reaching underneath the car
I've got a chance to live

     *

Frayed lace
Stunted soles

I never looked so close
At somebody's shoes

I never wondered what concrete tastes like
The way it seems to tremble when

Another truck pulls up
The killed engine

The immaculate
Cowboy boots

That Could Have Been Us

DAN CANON

"Stumpy's gonna breathe fire."

"Do what?"

"Yeah, Stumpy's gonna breathe fire. On stage."

A long pause. We stare at the road.

"What the fuck are you talkin' about?"

"Well, we don't exactly know how he's gonna do it yet, but there's that middle part in 'Godzilla' where it's just drums and shouting in Japanese and I think that's when he's gonna do it."

"Aw man, cool! But wait, *how's* he gonna do it?"

"Not sure yet. If you watch someone do that shit, Gene Simmons or one of those guys, they're just spittin' somethin' on a flame and it makes the flame get huge. They don't really *breathe* fire, y'know."

"Wait, hold up, so he's gotta play drums, handle an open flame, put somethin' flammable in his mouth, and then...well, let's stop there. How?"

Another long pause. A swig of biting, sterile, bottom-shelf bourbon. I swerve to avoid a skunk.

"I dunno. This wasn't really my idea."

"Jesus god. He'll kill us all. You know that, right? Jesus. He's gonna kill us. He's fuckin' insane."

I spent the rest of the hour-and-a half-drive from Louisville to Lexington trying to calm the nerves of Billy the Road Guy, whose last name no one knew, but who could carry an entire half-stack cabinet under his right arm. The logistics of fire-breathing were a minor problem, but Stumpy was a solid drummer and had the limb independence to do what was needed with one hand as long as someone handed him an open flame. We figured out you could light regular drum mallets, the Energizer bunny kind, and keep them going for a while. He was unlikely to kill us with just those.

Then there was the question of the flammable substance; the one that Stumpy (not his real nickname, let alone his name) would actually blow onto the open flame. Evolution had worked well enough to keep any of us from suggesting gasoline. But kerosene was seriously discussed, because, as I recall it, we had solicited opinions from area musicians who did it in the '60s, and that's what they said they used. He *could* kill us, or at least himself, with kerosene.

It's possible our elders were lying about the kerosene. And even if not, the utter disregard their ilk had for life and limb is legendary. We figured the ones who were left to talk about it couldn't be killed by conventional means. These are people who used to drink all day, take a handful of amphetamines, play a set, puke blood in the green room for fifteen minutes, try to fuck somebody else's girlfriend for another five minutes, play another set, and drink at the bar the rest of the night, all with a face full of open cold sores and a persistent ringing in the ears that would drive most rational mammals to serious self-harm. Such stubborn vitality could not have been drowned in a little kerosene. Perhaps we could survive it too.

Yet another problem is that Stumpy was, in fact, fuckin' insane, or you might say *different* in the way that people who spend countless hours pounding things with sticks are often *different*. His exploits were legendary by then, stories having accumulated from seven or eight bands, including an anarchist punk band, and an avant-garde outfit called Billy Graham's Pants. We had to break it to him, a grown man, that ham did not come from a bird. He once tried to cook ramen, but aborted the mission upon seeing steam, because "the WATER is on *FIRE!*" Our bass player, a normally soft-spoken, hulking mountain of a man who read Kierkegaard and drank naked-lady-labeled rum between sets, convinced him it would be a terrific idea to write a sci-fi rock opera about time-traveling, thirty-foot-tall jaguars (which he actually tried to do for about six months and gave up). You get the picture. We, his dear friends, have not let him forget any of this for even a moment of the last twenty years, but only because we managed to live that long. If there was one of us who had the capacity to kill the entire band all at once, it was Stumpy.

We eventually figured out you could make a pretty big fireball with a swig of Everclear (that's essentially pure-grain alcohol, for the uninitiated). But while it was one thing to hand him the gift of fire in the middle of a song, it was quite another to do that *and* get 190-proof liquid into his mouth without tripping over our own collective dick. So it was decided that he would simply hold the alcohol in his mouth for the entire song. This gave rise to another problem that was considered and quickly ignored: Stumpy was a fragile, anemic, Baptist-wedding-going, two-beers-and-pour-me-in-a-cab-brand lightweight.

But even with all that foreknowledge, we didn't stop to consider—*seriously* consider—that this fire-breathing stunt, performed in shallow honky-tonks in the Midwest and upper South, might actually kill us all. The thought of Stumpy's liver pickling on stage, of his head exploding, of him recreating the opening of *Apocalypse Now* in, say, the 1,000-square-foot River House Bar and Grille in Vevay, Indiana—these were not thoughts that provoked an acceptable, healthy level of dread. We were in our early twenties and could never die.

Or if we could, we didn't seem to care. Indeed, it was miraculous that we had not been killed already. None of us were really into drugs, but I was in a phase of drinking vodka like a Siberian housewife. I was almost in a dozen bar fights, all of which I escaped, but any one of which could have ended my life at a time when I weighed in at maybe 120 pounds. Most nights, the bass player, totally looped on naked-lady-rum, would end up taunting the biggest, dumbest guy in the room by the third set. We'd had foreign objects chucked at us, been chased out of parking lots by biker gangs, been stranded in the middle of nowhere, in the middle of the night, not sure how we got there. We were depressed, we were happy to be depressed, and we could have just as easily driven the band van off a cliff as gone to the next gig. And yet, like our predecessors, we lived. In defiance of any concept of karma or an omniscient, just God, we lived.

Lexington, where the fire-breathing incident occurred, is not like Louisville, and not like most Kentucky towns. It is a special combination of hypersexualized Greek life, horse gambling, bourbon, and old-school KKK bar brawlers. It is, therefore, a fine place to experiment with all kinds of terrible ideas. The club we were booked at had high ceilings, and it seemed a good place to try out the fire, because who knows? Maybe a couple of the sorority girls would get a kick out of it and be willing to talk to us. Maybe some big-time record producer would be in town to do some horse trading. Maybe we'd just give a handful of clubgoers something to remember.

Blue Öyster Cult's "Godzilla," as we played it, was about five minutes long, so Stumpy had to hold that fire water in his mouth for three and a half minutes. I finish my guitar solo. Time for drums, shouting in Japanese, and Stumpy to let loose.

My Japanese sounds like white-kid-from-Indiana Japanese, but no one in this Lexington bar knows or cares. I'm still at the mic, and I feel a blast of heat just over my right shoulder. Stumpy blows early, because his perception of time had been drastically altered by the first drop of weapons-grade moonshine to touch his tongue. It occurs to me for the first time that I'm very close to the drums, I've got a lot of hair, and I've got a lot of flammable product in my hair. But no, the heat is gone, I haven't been immolated, I will have no legendary disfigurement. Still, I smell something—something that isn't quite right.

I look over at the bass player, who is staring in at the ceiling with his mouth open. This wasn't unusual for him, but he wore an unmistakable look of horror that I hadn't seen before.

There had been an event there the week before. Some kind of Kentucky-meets-Mardi-Gras, syncretistic-frat-party horror show. Purple and yellow crepe streamers were taped all over the ceiling, hanging not so low as to be touched without a ladder, but low enough to be reached by a ball of fire. Some half-deflated balloons were up there, too.

The first time I look up to see any of this, I see thin, patchy lines of flame crawling up the drooping vines of streamers. The purple and yellow had been replaced by a brilliant orange in at least four different places. Two or three balloons burst from the heat. The whole ceiling was about to go up.

One rule of live performance is that you never, ever stop a song. It's a stupid rule, but there are stupid rules in every profession, and you have to live by them even if you know how stupid they are, or there's no way to know you're doing anything right. So we keep going. I make my way behind the drums to shout in Billy the Road Guy's ear to get the club manager. It smells like a still back there. Billy is frantically looking for a fire extinguisher or *something, anything to put this fucking fire out*, and doesn't pay any attention to me.

I amble back to the mic, expecting to die, or to have to get out of there in a hurry, or at least to be in a lot of trouble, but not really knowing what to do other than finish the song somehow.

At the time, it seemed a decent way to die, if that's what had to happen. I wasn't twenty-seven yet, but close enough. The music education we got in the Midwest mostly came from MTV, and was just enough to be dangerous. We had learned enough about Jimi and Janis to know that they were cool people who died at the cool age of twenty-seven doing something cool, but not quite enough to know that they asphyxiated on their own puke, which might have made it seem less cool. Maybe not. No matter; we started playing in bands around the same time as the explosive death of Kurt Cobain, a death which eclipsed all others for a time. To our testosterone-addled brains, blowing your own head off with a shotgun was not the final yelp of a pitiful, confused creature in so much pain that it no longer wishes to exist, but rather the climactic, dignified demise of a rock icon.

By the time I look up again, all that's left of what I was sure was going to be a four-alarm inferno is now condensed into one radiating, tiny globe.

It looks like a child's planetarium nestled itself in among the balloons, no more a threat than that. It's not enough to set off the sprinkler system that this club doesn't have, nor to warrant a claim with an insurer that it also doesn't have (assuming damage from an inebriated human flamethrower is covered by any policy in the first place, which I doubt).

We watch. A piece of crepe streamer is still glowing orange. Then it's not. It's black, because the ceiling is painted black, and most everything up there is black. There's smoke, but it's gone in a few seconds. Some of the balloons survived. Flakes of ash float onto Stumpy's ride cymbal, and are bounced back into the air, dispersing into a million tiny pieces, only visible in the beam of stage light, and now those pieces settle somewhere unseeable, unknowable. It's like nothing ever happened. Or if it did, it didn't matter. Or if it mattered, it was only to us.

We finish the gig in record time, what with the drummer playing everything at double speed and all. The stunt hadn't gotten us laid. It didn't get us paid any extra. No one else noticed that the ceiling was briefly ablaze. I'm not sure they knew Stumpy was breathing fire. At that moment, I'm not sure if Stumpy himself knew. We load up and drive home.

On another long drive back to Louisville, after another, less-noteworthy gig, we hear the news. A hundred people died at a Great White concert in Rhode Island. The pyrotechnics went wrong, and ignited the walls, which were made of soundproofing foam. Our club's ceiling and walls were not insulated with this foam, which is why I'm able to write this. The foam in the Rhode Island club had a chemical in it that not only made it highly flammable, but toxic to breathe, too. People were climbing over each other trying to get away from the stage, making stacks of bodies, blocking the exits. At the same time, poisonous black smoke was billowing from the walls. A lung full of that stuff meant a dose of a powerful paralytic agent, which meant you couldn't move anymore, and if you couldn't move, all you had left to do was lay there and wait to burn to death. Most of the victims died that night, but some held on for a couple of weeks, wasting away in a burn unit. It was about as ghastly a scene as one could possibly imagine.

"Goddamn, dude," Billy said to me. "That could have been us."

In the years since then, Stumpy's brain has been sucked out of the airlock of rationality and into the empty void of twenty-four-hour news propaganda, leaving him to pound out daily Facebook screeds against whoever the enemy *du jour* is. His wife and (now grown) kids still love him, somehow. Billy the Road Guy has worked in a potato chip factory for more than ten years. He is still unusually strong, but got diabetes and went blind for a couple of days. He's better now, but he doesn't get out much. The bassist teaches philosophy to college students. He's got a door with a nameplate, $200,000 in student loans, and a bunch of cats that he dotes on in a fastidious, grandfatherly way.

Some of the victims' families still hold Great White's original front man, Jack Russell, responsible for what happened in Rhode Island. Russell is not as famous as his canine namesake, but he is still making music, still touring, still there in the spotlight, for audiences that are getting older and smaller every year. Russell still gets interviewed about the fire. He's done benefit concerts for the victims. I'd guess he thinks about it every day and has nightmares about it every night.

On the other hand, Great White's guitar player, Ty Longley, died a gruesome, tragic, glorious death on stage in Rhode Island—one that is still commemorated every February, almost twenty years later. He initially escaped the club, but in an act of courage, no doubt born of the special brand of immortality all touring musicians possess (until they don't), he went back in for his guitar. Most days it seems obvious who out of that band got the better end of the Rhode Island deal; some days, not so much.

As for me, I went from a long-haired, skinny, pockmarked rock god to a bald, slouching, middle-aged trial lawyer. I have kids. I have a wife. I have a house with dogs in it. I have a minivan. I, along with my bandmates and many people in the Lexington club that night, got to have many things that people in the Rhode Island club didn't ever get a chance to have, which doesn't seem fair. My tolerance, my temper, and my libido have all subsided. It's a respectable, quiet life that I could not have imagined for myself twenty years ago; one without much blood, vodka, or fire. Most of the time, I'm glad to be living it. Some days, not so much. On those days, I sing an old song to remember that purposeful fire-breathing beast behind me, and what history shows again and again.

Drift

JOY PRIEST

after Robert Frost's "Directive"

It becomes too much for us,
so, we take a dip. Ride
     aimless down this parkway
parting unruly brush. Nature

     so heavy it feels, at any moment,
ready to erupt & absorb
     this silly city men have made.
We are magnificent & overhead

     the trees crowd, like a mob,
into canopy. The butt of his boxed Chevy
     sways across double-yellow bars—
eroded lanes cutting

     east-to-west on our side
of the city—Beech
     & Cypress, 22nd & 18th
where it turns into Dixie,

     past Park Hill's dull yellow brick,
its clotheslines and identical yards,
     building after numbered building
crossing the glass globe of my eye,

     past the hair store, Grand Mkt.,
the apts. where my father lived
     when I met him, & the loud teal
awning of Shark's Fish & Chicken.

I sit shotgun sans seat belt.
Tonight, knot-gutted —that tell
          for fear. Maniac leant
behind the wheel, eyes nearly closed,

in his gut: a fistful of pills,
          tiny yellow footballs. Before
he slams into that giant pin oak
          down the pkwy, before the steam

          & the rust flakes floating
through the one beam
          of that insistent headlight,
that streetlamp giving up

          to the dark, something telling me
to get out. When I leave
          his grey Caprice, I step out of
a dimension, a place in my youth

          I can't return to. How quick
the fire turns to ash as I hand
          the smoke to him. He is pulling away.
The cigarillo is slipping through

          his dangled fingers to join the ground
like every ending thing: he's done
          enough to escape our streets—
numbered, or named for the trees.

Abecedarian for Alzheimer's

JOY PRIEST

Angel was my pappaw's girlfriend when he died.
Back there, in my memory, I hear my mother fussing about
condoms & *AIDS!* She is saying, *The girl is only 25, & Black!* My
daddy, amused at the irony of racism, whispering to me: *He's at his
end anyway.* Angel was stripping at Déjà Vu when he moved her into the
front bedroom & this is where I began to realize what, precisely, was
going on: He couldn't remember me, but by then he was forgetting who
he was too. Outside the club, next to our world famous horseracing track, the
infamous sign read: *Win-Place-Show Bar | 99 Pretty Girls & 1 Ugly One!* A
jab at Angel—their only dark-skinned dancer. She mystified them with her
kaleidoscope of color contacts & quick weave. They loved her *equine* legs. I
loved her for telling my secret loud, for making a messy joke of him & my
mother the way I felt they had made a mess of me. After Angel moved in I
never saw him again. My mother avoided his street. She could not get
over the hypocrisy: How he'd disowned her when I was born, then made her
promise not to speak of my blackness, my father, to me. Buried hole of
quiet lies they dug for years before it opened beneath the two of us &
ruined everything. Maybe my mother envied Angel because she
saw the truth of him out & when he began forgetting
to hate us, to put his white hood on every day, Angel
used him the proper way. I like to think of her as
Veritas, the goddess at the bottom of that empty
well, naked & holding a hand mirror. Or maybe it was me, a
xeric un-blooming thing down there beneath them. I had, for
years, been taught to live that way: Black, unassuming,
zipped up in history—a disease not even progress can cure.

God of the Motorcade (2005)

JOY PRIEST

In Louisville, from a sidewalk-
turned-sideline on West Broadway,
I catch my beloved,

     absent for weeks now,

leading a cortège of Chevelles through the chaos
of revelers,
     as earlier that day the children
led their handmade floats around a grade-school
     Derby parade.

     As he comes toward me,

so too does a throat-dark woman
carrying past the scent of coconut,
her naked breasts glisten, slick
     as the skin of his convertible coupe.

My eyes—lit up at him—know
     why he chooses this very spot to turn
          the chain of revving beasts
     through a slow U:

          picture the Nian at New Year, now
     his headlights flooding across
my red velour Rocawear dress
     & for a moment you can see
          I am the one. Rumor has it

the beast's weakness
     is an aversion to loud noises,
          fear of the color red.

We are all too familiar with this combination,
myths that we are. Even this night

on the main thoroughfare of River City, splitting our side
in two, a few of us will become

legend. I hear a girl say *there he is!* (my lover
who is also her lover, I see). I watch

a boy dance with sharp & ancient movements
to Lil' Boosie on the roof of an old Buick.

Someone' daddy calling out *Redbone* to me
from behind a pit, thick with smoke
            & the end of an animal. The tail

          of the monster that keeps him from me, always
out of reach, whips away & evanesces
at the bend on 18th street.

Horsepower

JOY PRIEST

Offseason.
      Before the racetrack opens,

I step through the threshold
of my back door.
           Stable-side.

A dove takes off from a nest
tucked into the corner
of the porch awning, glides
through my known world
which I can see
in its entirety from my top step:

                  the twin steeples
& emerald roofs just past
our garage,

          a horse practicing
its start out of the gate.

     Only Longfield —
that Avenue rounding
the perimeter of the pill-shaped track
where the red & white & green flags
ripple from balconies & my neighbors
sell horchata in Styrofoam cups, street tacos
in paper baskets w/ cilantro & lime —
Only Longfield & a chain-link fence

separates the horses' air from mine,

they work the loop of that circular mile
making everyone's living
                    except their own —
the motors of our economy.
Beyond the spires
is a larger world I do not know
exists. A mile West, in my line
of vision, is a family
I do not know
I have.

           In that corner of the city
—separating from the land like a cell in mitosis,
straining across the Ohio River
to the north—

my great aunt, black matriarch, rocks
on her blue porch

& my father, my father,

just a couple of blocks away from her, coos
my baby brother into sleep
while his new wife flours

the wings of a flightless bird.

But all I know
for now is my grandfather
the white one,

& I know my mother, who I hear now, roaring
home from work in her muscle car.

& wait—

           I know the horses,

the horses & their restless minds.

Derby

JOY PRIEST

First Saturday in May. My mother wrestles my hair into two ponytails.
The only day of the year she bothers. The upsweep of skin

pulls my face into a grin. Special occasion
barrettes molded into the white, plastic body of a horse
gallop behind me at the tip of my braids as I race
the stretch of our narrow alley street, shouting
into the shimmering cars' mirrored windows
            through cartoon-sized teeth:

                PARK HERE! TEN DOLLARS!

                        *

Eight years old and I am a professional.

Up early to greet the regulars:

            Mr. Whitlock, Black Lincoln Town Car.
            Mr. Crouch, Red Topless Corvette.

I usher the expensive machines
into the VIP spaces
of our carport,
                    pander through the heavy hands
                    dropped on my freshly-parted scalp. All day long,
                    up & down Cliff Ave.,

I am my mother's gimmick,

                    reeling in the big bettors,

slipping stiff money into envelopes
giving directions to the entrance
in my tiny voice, picking
the sure horse, selling
plots of our yard and lemonade

to orange-tinted men sweating
through linen, their nameless
women under gaudy hats . . .

*

We memorize their faces
from scratchy lawn chairs,
beneath a mellow blimp
humming through the sky.

And then the streets empty.

The announcer's voice echoes,
blankets our roofs. A distant Oz.

Grills warming, beers hissing,
crowd buzzing like a radio
between stations. Waiting

for the races to let out,
for our customers to stumble back
from that fortress we never saw
inside of,

we argued
garage-to-garage,
placed the real bet:
                    which of us would be the first to go.

From Grandstands to Infield

GWEN NIEKAMP

It is the 142nd running of the Kentucky Derby, and the Churchill Downs infield is a city of seersucker: 70,000 people in twenty-six muddy acres. The sky is overcast, a rocky start to spring, but still pastel is in. Everywhere I look: posy pinks and ditsy florals and beachy aquas. I fit in with my Derby dress; it's mint green with little pink-brown horses on it. I know it's childish for a woman nearing twenty-six, but the colors are right. ("You look like a mint julep," said Anna when I tried it on in the dressing room of that Nulu boutique. "I just want to eat you up!") I'm glad I wore it with sneakers. The rain has let up, but the mud has laid claim to heels and flip flops, one here, one there. I keep to the paths, shouldering my way through the crowd. Betting lines frazzle into mobs, and thank god I have the TVG app. When I'm not paying attention, my little flower fascinator catches on another woman's hat. We laugh as we disentangle ourselves and we grasp shoulders and tell each other that we're beautiful. "Win big today," I tell her instead of goodbye.

I should let on that I'm a little bit buzzed. My friends and I snuck liquor into the track in colostomy bags; we smuggled them past security in the cups of our bras. Anna brought a safety pin, and we pierce the bags when we're ready for slow-streaming shots. We squeeze them dry for each other, holding them above outstretched tongues and playfully letting the liquor stray to our lips and philtrums and chins. Just a few drops here and there on our faces, but still we say, "Hey, watch it, bitch! Just kidding. I love you. Do it again." We are proud that we like bourbon—that we *actually* like bourbon and that we like it neat. We've all traded stories about the first time we tasted it. Usually we were very young and sick and our grandparents gave us a mouthful to treat our sore throats. "We grew up drinking bourbon!" yells Anna to the bachelor party from out of town that has settled on picnic blankets next to us. They laugh at us for our colostomy bags; we laugh at them for paying jacked-up prices for Old Forester Mint Julep Ready-to-Serve Cocktail.

The favorite is Nyquist, but I won't bet him. I learned from my dad. "Where's the fun in that?" he'd say. "The payout is pennies." But I don't think it pays off to bet the longshot either, however promising he looks, however lively his tail as he parades to the paddock, however mesmerizing the sway of his hips as he enters the starting gate. I choose horses with odds between 10- and 20-1. I want Gun Runner. I want Creator. I want Danzing Candy. They're not safe bets, but they're not too risky either.

Dad goes risky. He won big, big, big in 2005. He put seventy-some-odd bucks to win on Giacomo, whose odds were 50 to 1. That night, to celebrate, Dad took us out for pizza at the now-defunct Giacomo's in Germantown. We were all happy, even my mom, but that was one of only a handful of big wins and their marriage didn't last much longer.

Only men enter the porta potty races. My girlfriends and I watch them scramble on top of the line of those teal shit boxes, then take a beer can to the neck and tumble off the slick roofs, land on their backs. When they get up, they are mud-drenched and they threaten nearby women with hugs. Sometimes the women fall on their faces as they try to escape. My friends and I back away. "Retreat! Retreat!" yell Anna and I. We head back to the picnic blanket.

I'm lying on the picnic blanket with my forearm draped over my eyes when my phone bleets. It's my brother, texting to say that he is also in the infield. I go to find him at the third turn.

The crowd is this: bleary-eyed white women in cocktail dresses swaying and singing along to music from Bluetooth speakers—there's a lot of John Mellenkamp; a man laying his blazer down in the mud for a giggling woman to walk on—"see, I told you I was a gentleman," he says; couples tonguing; women sitting on men's laps; people rummaging around in their coolers for pepperoni and homemade egg salad sandwiches; people sleeping; people with vomit running down the collars of their clothes.

I find my brother and his friends clustered under a tent. He separates himself when he sees me and tells me that Dad hooked him up with infield passes too. When we were younger, our family used to have box seats, and my mom, my dad, Jamie, and I would sit in them together. On the way to the track, we'd pick up Arby's sandwiches and we'd sit on them in the box seats to keep them warm until lunch. Our box was on the far right side of the grandstands, the last one in the row—this was before the renovation—and Jamie and I would look over the railing into the sea of people below. We got the idea to take our curly fries, dangle them over the edge, and aim them at the wide brims of Derby hats. We cheered, then ducked, whenever we landed a fry amidst feathers and flowers. Before I turned double digits, we lost the box. Dad still comes through with infield passes though. He knows a guy who knows a guy who gives them out for free.

"Have you met my date?" asks Jamie, pursing his lips. He nods to the other side of the tent, toward a clean-cut college boy in seersucker who's clinking mint julep glasses with two women. The boy catches us looking and blows Jamie a kiss.

"Where'd you find him?" I ask.

"Grindr." Then he drops his voice, "He's the worst kind of gay—*Republican*. God, I have to get out of the fucking South."

I offer Jamie the consolation of a colostomy bag and head back to my friends.

When we lost the box in the grandstands, I started to resent this place. Dad dragged me and Jamie along to Churchill Downs every Sunday of the fall and spring meets—and in off-season, we had to go to Off-Track Betting instead. Back then, people could smoke inside either place, and our clothes would smell filthy after just an hour. We begged to leave but Dad promised us soft-serve ice cream and another two bucks each to put on a horse if we could just stop bitching. Jamie and I were often the only kids, and I was almost always the only girl. I hated that all of Dad's friends made the same joke when they saw us. Cigars wagging out of their mouths, they'd say, "Hey, Billy! Good thing your kids got their looks from their mama." Sometimes I had to go to the track on weekdays too. Dad had a backside pass in those days, and he would wake me up 90 minutes earlier than I needed to wake up for school so he could watch the morning workouts before he dropped me off. I was cold, my legs bare in my school jumper, my shoes and socks damp from walking through the morning dew which had settled on the grass, and once I watched a horse fall. The moment plays in slow motion for me every now and then. The horse's coat ripples on impact, purpled in the weird dawn light, and the exercise rider goes sailing into the guardrail, which catches her like she's a piece of laundry hung to dry. It is amazing and it is terrible.

I didn't go to the track much in high school, and by college, I'd go with friends, not with my dad. We'd go for Downs After Dark, night racing events aimed at millennials. We danced in the paddock to DJs, took pictures in photo booths, bought tacos from food trucks, and had long discussions in which we tried to determine the order in which we'd marry. We didn't watch much racing, but I do remember once putting money on a race that ended in a dead heat. I had bet one of the winning horses, and Anna had bet the other, and when the race was too close to call—something that rarely happens—we jumped into each other's arms shrieking, "We won! We won!"

I remember it so well because I bet very little in college. After my parents' divorce, my dad rented a storage unit for the stuff that wouldn't fit in his little apartment. On a school break, I went rummaging in there for some of my things, and what I found instead were garbage bags full of losing tickets. Some were my dad's, but I guessed that some, the ones from the '60s and '70s, might have been my paternal grandfather's. He'd liked to play the ponies too. Each bag was full enough that I could stick my hand inside, churn the tickets around, and imagine I was touching real bills. Five dollars here, ten there. This is all to say that the track is a place I've come to associate with family—my dad, his dad—but am I the first in line to also associate it with pain? Even now as I walk through the infield on the day that Churchill Downs is the most crowded, I feel some sort of ownership of it. Or rather, I feel like this place owes itself to me, to my brother, and to my mom. It is a toxic kind of love, unhealthy and angry but real, that I have for the track.

It's post time when I get back to my friends after spending some time with my brother, which means it's time to sing, "My Old Kentucky Home." The storm clouds open up just as the music begins, but my friends and I won't run for cover, not today, so we grab our picnic blanket, a faded full-size bedsheet, and drape it over ourselves, trying to fit all eight of us underneath. One of my shoulders goes uncovered, and it prickles with goosebumps in the rain. Together, we belt that song, wind whipping through the sheet, mud covering our shoes, alcohol in our veins, and I know it's shameful to admit, melodramatic even, but when 100,000-odd voices join in, that song collapses into a low hum. The sound of it brings me to tears.

When My Old Kentucky Home Was New to Me

AARON ROSENBLUM

I moved to Louisville, Kentucky around the first of May in 2005. On the sixth, a Friday and the eve of the 131st running of the Kentucky Derby, I performed for the first time as a member of a long-running Louisville music collective at a potluck and party on a small urban farm incongruously nestled between a golf course, a well-to-do subdivision, and an interstate highway. The instant invitation into the band, the welcoming atmosphere of the farm party, and the introduction that night to now-longtime friends all seemed to justify the fairly sudden and somewhat arbitrary decision I had made a few months earlier to leave my jobs and community in Massachusetts and move to Louisville. I don't remember anyone at the party making much mention of that day's Kentucky Oaks or the next day's Derby, but I gathered that I had arrived in Louisville at a generally festive time of year.

The next day, a friend took me with her to a family Derby party held at her folks' house in the suburban Fern Creek neighborhood. The weather was perfect, sunny and warm. As I would later find out is the custom, the festivities began hours before the race. Siblings, cousins, aunts and uncles, nieces and nephews played games, grilled, drank beer, and bet on the undercard races. I felt a little out of place but was made entirely welcome. Not to say I had moved to Kentucky with any great interest in the Derby, but I was glad to be invited and certainly didn't want to miss out on the spectacle and the chance to observe the folkways of Louisvillians on their big unofficial holiday.

After the undercard races had been run, a change came over the gathering. Everyone assembled on the deck, where a television had been moved from inside the house so we could watch the race in the sunshine. Anticipation and celebratory tension—akin to the seventh inning stretch during a World Series game or the pause before the announcement of the Oscar for Best Picture—filled the space. I soon learned that this pre-race anticipatory gap would be filled not with "Take Me Out to the Ballgame" but with the state song, performed live at the track. As the song began I realized that not only were the crowds at Churchill Downs and gathered on the deck around me singing along, but that Kentuckians in their homes, at bars, and perhaps in exile all over the world, were simultaneously singing along to Stephen Foster's 1853 ballad "My Old Kentucky Home." Neat!

I knew Stephen Foster's music from childhood music lessons, Looney Tunes, and any number of other sources of the American cultural canon that I had encountered in my then twenty-three years. If I knew "My Old Kentucky Home" at all, I surely didn't know the lyrics by heart. So I listened rather than joining in, and heard something I wasn't expecting and that I was totally unprepared to hear.

With the exception of my friend and possibly a few others, the assembled partygoers were singing not the current, official lyrics, but an earlier version of "My Old Kentucky Home." In that version, I heard a group of white southerners—outdoors and in full daylight—belt out:

The sun shines bright on my old Kentucky home / 'tis summer –

If you know the song, in any form, you know the image that follows—a group of joyful people. But in this version of the lyrics, those people are Black. More to the point, they are enslaved. And the word used to identify them is a racist slur. And while this particular slur has mostly fallen out of use since the early twentieth century, I couldn't and can't imagine anyone would have trouble identifying it as a harmful pejorative term, in 2005 or 2020.

I was stupefied. Had I just heard what I thought I heard? That language? Not just uttered, but sung out loud, in a modern city, in a state that never even left the Union? I was by no means unaware of the very real racism of the Northeast, where I came from, or on the West Coast, where I had lived for a time as well. In New York and California, Massachusetts and Maine, I had heard plenty of racist and bigoted language, usually uttered by groups of white men in their private gatherings. I had observed the racial dynamics between the white, well-to-do families of my New York City-suburb hometown and the often Black and brown housekeepers, landscapers, and service industry employees who worked for them. And in what little time I had spent traveling in the South in the years prior I had seen more than enough Confederate flags on shirts, bumpers, and flagpoles to get the drift.

I should say that I expect lots of folks will not be shocked in the least by any of this, and I admit this is a story of my own naiveté as much as anything else. But up to that point I had never seen or heard anything like this brazen, outright, and above all proud hollering of really vile racist language in full public view. What's more, the people at this party weren't wearing and perhaps wouldn't wear a Confederate flag shirt, and they were standing in blue Jefferson County, where even those precincts that went for John McCain over Barack Obama three years later only did so by a handful of votes.

My friend must have seen my slack-jawed, blood-drained face. She explained that while she strongly disagreed with them, these were the "original lyrics" and her family members were doing their traditional Kentucky thing, wrong as it was. I make no judgment of my friend here. She may or may not have called out this tradition in her family before or since, and it's not for me to say whether she should have. And though I was a somewhat incompetent member of my own family at that time, the years since have taught me what it takes to really love family, and what that love must tolerate. But what we must bear in order to look upon our mothers and fathers, brothers and sisters, our children, and those we hold dear is different from what we must bear in the community beyond our families and our back yards.

I attended my fair share of Derby parties in the following years until recently deciding that I can't abide another. All of them were more than pleasant, and none featured recitations of those earlier lyrics to "My Old Kentucky Home." But every single one, forthrightly or ironically, participated willingly in the farce that is the main marker of Derby as holiday for Louisvillians and Kentuckians: that there is room in the "sport of kings," beyond the stables, for the peasants.

That the unwashed are welcome for one day, that those in power deign to allow us access, to pretend to their pretenses without being laughed out of the grandstand. That those trapped in the American credit economy, or the student loan or health care debt trap, in a state that observes the federal minimum wage of $7.25 an hour even now, who can ill afford to clothe themselves and their families, are encouraged to blow money on seersucker and sundresses, on fantastical hats and jackass slacks, on bets in a loaded, fractious, exploitative game where the real money is made not in six-dollar trifectas but in owning, training, and running horses to death, mistreating undocumented workers or funding the politics of hatred and exclusion of which they are a primary target, exploiting jockeys and leaving them unprotected and uninsured when injured, making grand and absurd marketing deals for the "Official Leave-in Conditioner of the 2020 Kentucky Derby," and selling an entire region on the idea that their pride should arise not from their own cultures and communities but from the darkest aspects of their racist past and present, from proximity to a momentary concentration of wealth so temporary that it can't even lift the neighborhoods mere yards away from Churchill Downs out of poverty. There is no doubt in my mind that it is the marketeer's chimera of "tradition" that provided the social cover for that anachronistic backyard rendition of Foster's racist lyrics, as it is the cover for so much else about Derby that ought not be accepted or acceptable.

While discussing these issues, a friend who has spent many years celebrating both Derby in Louisville and Mardi Gras in New Orleans pointed out to me that, though the mimicry of wealth is a Mardi Gras tradition too, that mimicry is explicitly, religiously intended as the mockery of wealth. The camel through the needle's eye and all that. But with Derby, with Louisville, there can be no mistaking the intentions of the craven forces that would desecrate the very architectural signature of Churchill Downs—its stately, historical twin spires, now dwarfed and obscured by luxury box sections housed in blankly industrial and casinoesque architecture—in the name of greater profits. The street-facing walls of those new sections are mostly devoid of windows, in a flat refusal to confront the surrounding neighborhoods and the realities of those who live near and with the track every day of the year, not just for two minutes on the first Saturday in May.

I see little evidence that there is anyone at the top of this sporting and cultural pyramid scheme with an interest in the Kentucky customs and culture I have grown to love and that have kept me here for most of the last fifteen years, or in any meaningful sense of civic pride or progress. There likely never has been, and I see little chance that there ever will be. The Derby party I attended in 2005 was my first, and it should have been my last. My old Kentucky home, good night.

Finding My Tribe

DAVID SERCHUK

Ten thousand.

That was, I was told, the total number of Jews in Louisville.

I heard this number so often it became a truism in my mind. There were only 10,000 of us, in a metro area of 1 million. That's one percent.

This number did not fill my heart with joy. One percent?! My god, that's not much, that's a minority of a minority. As if I didn't already feel isolated and alone.

You see, we had moved to Louisville in July 2010 from New York City. I am from the greater New York area, and am Jewish. That area is *so* Jewish all kids get the major Jewish holidays off from school. Outside of Israel it's likely the most Jewish place on the planet.

And I *loved* that about New York. I didn't feel like an outsider there.

Just between us, I didn't want to move to Louisville. It was under, how shall I say this, duress. My wife, Randi, is from Kentucky and after we had our daughter Stella in 2008 her old Kentucky homing device went off, calling her back to her people.

I was against such a move as all my friends, family, and professional contacts were in New York. Plus, I had a pretty good job at Forbes.com as a deputy editor. I could resist all arguments in favor of moving until … the Great Recession. I lost my job, couldn't find another one, our money started to pour, sieve-like, from our bank accounts and we had a big argument. Randi said no matter what, even if we stayed, she would never be happy in New York ever again.

She was depressed, I was depressed, I was worried our two-year old daughter was depressed and we decided to roll the dice on Louisville. I didn't know what it would offer. I didn't have any friends or family there. In time I would learn to say I didn't have any *people* there.

Randi is from Upton, Kentucky, which is about an hour from Louisville. It's a sweet little town, roughly 1,000 people big. Having said that, Upton was a big *hell no* from the both of us. If we were going to move to Kentucky it would have to be to its biggest city. And that meant Louisville.

Our first mission was to find a new place to live. Finding an apartment in New York is akin to crossing all nine circles of hell, only with brokers' fees. I expected much the same in Louisville. I was ready to hear I'd have to provide a deposit equal to one month's rent, and then first month's rent and last month's rent. This was simply how it was done in NYC. Our rent in NYC, by the way, was $1,600 per month; a comparative steal!

Imagine my shock when we called the first apartment complex on our list, Mallard Crossing, and got someone on the phone right away. They told us we'd need a deposit. *All right, here it comes*, I thought, *how much?* Two hundred dollars. It felt like Monopoly money. And water service was free.

Our rent, by the way, was $900 per month, a pittance. I later boasted about our sweet deal to new friends and they looked at me with pity; how'd we get *so* ripped off?

I drove all our things from New York to Louisville in a big U-Haul with a trailer in the back that held our tan Honda Accord and our two cats, Cromwell and Talisker.

The main office of Mallard Crossing was a grand plantation-style building with a big, broad porch and rocking chairs. I felt like I had stepped into the setting for, I don't know, *Cat on a Hot Tin Roof* or something.

Our movers showed up, three dudes in a red Mustang, all smoking. They were incredibly friendly, worked hard and fast, and were grateful for the adequate tip I gave them. Okay, maybe Louisville had some good points.

But the acres of asphalt around the complex depressed me. The lack of urban density also depressed me. In fact, it was easy to depress me right about then. I felt like I had nothing left of my life, other than my family. Which was a lot, and yet my sense of loss was palpable. But we had no choice other than to make it work in this strange new urban/suburban setting.

Stella was preschool age, and we immediately set to work finding her a placement for the upcoming year. In New York, again, this is a nightmarish decathlon-style exercise where you have to apply months in advance, they interview your toddler, and if they deign to accept you it will only cost $25,000 per year.

We called Jewish preschools, asking for tours. The friendly people on the other end were always more than happy to oblige, at our convenience, with tours and information. This was a nice change.

We toured the preschools at Keneseth Israel Congregation, The Temple, and Congregation Adath Jeshurun. We were shocked to learn these Jewish preschools were filled with non-Jewish children. In fact, they were about twenty-five percent Jewish. AJ was the highest, I believe, at thirty percent.

As we toured one of the schools I told the rabbi about how big an adjustment Louisville had been for me. "I mean, I've heard there are only 10,000 Jewish people here, total," I said.

He paused—rabbinically, of course—and answered: "Actually, the number is closer to 8,000."

Wait, I'd already lost 2,000 potential Jews since I got here? What did I do?

On the upside, we were something of a positive novelty in the local Jewish community. You see, Louisville's Jewish community has been shrinking for decades as the children of community members often travel to big urban centers like LA, Chicago and, you guessed it, New York to start careers and families. Some come back, but many don't.

I can't say AJ found room for us simply because we were a new Jewish family, but I also can't rule it out. Even though Louisville's preschool scene is, no doubt, less competitive than New York's, AJ was still a coveted place with a wait list. But somehow not for us. Stella was soon enrolled for the upcoming year, and the monthly tuition was only $800 a month. A bargain!

Now I had to work on building new business contacts and relationships. So, of course, I immediately pissed everyone off.

I had been an (unpaid) contributor to the *Huffington Post*. I decided to write a little humor piece comparing my new town with the old one.

The article ran on August 30, 2010 and was titled "Smackdown! New York vs. Louisville." I tried to poke light-hearted fun at the foibles of both towns. Boy, what a bust that was.

Here is my opening paragraph:

"As a newcomer to Louisville (that's in Kentucky) I can't help but compare it to my old stomping ground, New York City. Why did I move here? Should you care? Those, my friends, are questions that have no answer. Today I am just going to shoot from the hip and see how the River City stacks up against the Big Apple. Get out your scorecards!"

I compared and scored each city on things like the quality of the water, sports teams, friendliness, options for lodging, and food. Of all the things I wrote I think the paragraph about food hurt people in Louisville the most. Here it is:

New York has the best deli, bagels, pizza, Chinese food, Thai food, Indian food, Pakistani food passed off as Indian food, Italian food apart from pizza, and whatever it is they actually sell out of those pushcarts. Lamb? Rat?

Louisville has hot browns, good barbecue, Derby Pie and Chick-fil-A. I love Chick-fil-A, and New York has like one. Crazy, right? Crazy.

Advantage: New York.

At the end I said the cities tied. But I felt the need to end it on this additional, cheeky note:

"Okay, so let's call it a draw ... for now. I look forward to getting to know my new hometown more, so I can stack the deck one way or the other in the future. So be nice to me Louisville! Now onto less contentious matters: Wildcats or Cardinals? (For you New Yorkers: those are college teams.)"

The comments section in the article soon filled up, entirely from people in Louisville, most of whom were irritated by me. New Yorkers, of course, didn't care about anything I wrote.

Believe it or not the Louisville press soon noticed. The local online news source *Insider Louisville* wrote this sweet little piece, titled "HuffPost features Louisville in smack down with NYC; We suck."

You could say the article's writer, Terry Boyd, took my article personally: "Anyway, some hipster financial writer named David Serchuk has honored us by moving to the remote hinterland of Louisville ("that's in Kentucky, ha, ha, ha!") from Brooklyn. Clearly, we don't come off well in Serchuk's oh-so-clever Big Apple versus River City smackdown for *Huffington Post*."

Dude, I *did* say it was a tie!

Then there was a true tempest in a teapot. Michelle Jones, the author of the popular Louisville food blog "Consuming Louisville," wrote up a pointed repost explaining, quite patiently, there was a good deal more to Louisville's cuisine scene than Chick-fil-A. The worst part? She didn't seem angry, just disappointed. So disappointed.

(Today I say *screw* Chick-fil-A and its homophobic sandwiches.)

The local free alternative news outlet, the *Louisville Eccentric Observer*, also wrote about my (unpaid) *Huffington Post* article, although LEO noted I did have a point about Louisville's lame-ass public transportation system.

Then Gabe Bullard, a journalist at Louisville's local NPR affiliate WFPL, wrote up an online item titled, "Man Moves to Louisville, Internet Notices." The man, of course, was me. He ended it by welcoming me to Louisville, and to the internet.

The truth was, I felt pretty bad about coming across like an arrogant New York prick in my new hometown. I might be from the New York area, but big city swagger has never been my style.

But here's the cool part. Although I believed I'd infuriated the journalism establishment from the get-go the strong, and in many ways, negative reaction from the article proved to be a blessing in disguise.

After we signed Stella up at AJ, we became members. We wanted to be a part of the Jewish community. It was a way of bringing some calm and familiarity to our lives amidst this massive and in some ways painful set of changes.

And whom did I meet at AJ? Michelle Jones. She was a longtime member, as was her partner Belinda Setters. Despite a frisson of initial tension, we broke ice and bread at a post-service lunch. We soon became fast friends.

Next, I rolled the dice and called Gabe Bullard. We met for a coffee, exchanged information, and became decent acquaintances. Over the next few years I wrote a handful of articles for him, and even won some awards for these pieces.

It took me a bit longer to work up the courage to contact Terry Boyd, as he was the most pissed-off. But when I did, we hit it off, too. In time I eventually became a staff writer for *Insider Louisville*. Several years later I later brought that initial article up to Terry and I swear to you he had no idea what I was talking about.

Also, yeah, Louisville's Jewish community might not be a big one, but it's big enough. Sometimes more than big enough.

On October 27, 2018, an anti-Semitic madman stormed into the Tree of Life synagogue in Pittsburgh, killing eleven and injuring far more.

The reaction from Louisville's Jewish community and its allies was immediate and amazing. There was an evening vigil at Temple Shalom. The building was so full people waited in line to get in.

Once inside I saw people from every walk of life, every color. Maybe the room was only 25 percent Jewish, but this time I saw this as a source of support and strength. As a Jew I am used to being hated and misunderstood. That night I saw clearly how many people believe that what happens to one of us happens to all of us. It's something most Jews understand. But it was amazing to see people use this mindset to rally around us.

This vigil was followed by an open service at Adath Jeshurun. By this time, we'd made a group of new friends, many of whom attend Highland Baptist Church. I was visibly moved to see so many non-Jewish friends gather round us for one reason alone: to show us we are supported and valued.

Speaking of love, when Samuel, our second child, was born we knew there was only one couple we wanted for his godparents: Michelle and Belinda. And they are the best godmothers a little boy could have. They shower this little child with love and, of course, gifts. (Stella had also been a flower girl at their wedding.)

As we approach our tenth year in Louisville, so much has changed. My fear has given way to acceptance and the understanding that disruption is simply the rule. I can fight it, but I can't beat it. I will never not miss my old friends and family, but I now know there are wonderful new people all around us. Together we make a new tribe, some of whom are of *the* Tribe, some not.

So though there are only 8,000 Jews in Louisville, at most, I'm okay with that. I'd like to meet them all. And everyone else here, too.

Boom, Bust, Boom, Clap, Boom

SVETLANA BINSHTOK

In Old Louisville there is a small windowless warehouse tucked behind a pill dispensary with a big smiling orange sun on the sign. You probably wouldn't see it as you drove down Sixth Street unless the afternoon line of customers had already started to snake through the black tar parking lot. During the day a roofing company operated out of the space, storing slate shingles, sheets of copper, and spare tools, but on special nights the heavy roll-up doors were lowered, the roofing equipment cleared, and then the music started.

By 4 a.m., the dense air sagged with the musk of panting dancers and the dust that they shuffled off the concrete floor. Laughter and shrieks echoed above the bass. At night, you probably wouldn't notice the warehouse is even there, unless you patiently followed the rhythmic thumping and looked for ravers in repose strewn around the small parking lot, taking a PLUR break and catching their breath. Or if you knew what to look for.

In 2009, the annual Zombie Walk took over the Highlands on August 29 as it did every year. I moved to Louisville less than a week earlier and so I spent the evening alone at Heine Brothers on Longest Avenue, fruitlessly looking for a job and doing what little freelance writing work I managed to scrounge up. The barista made the final call—you don't have to go home, but you can't stay here.

On the street, a tall woman with very short, bright red hair yelled out to me. "Hey! You!" she said pointing at me. "Want to go to a party?"

Marea recently returned to Louisville from living in Chicago for almost ten years. Her own music career stalled and she came home to where she grew up as a '90s raver. While she was regrouping, she also had an itch.

On that sweltering August night, in the back of a white truck, with a zombie in a feathered mullet, I went to my first rave. A couple weeks later I helped my new friends throw a warehouse party.

What do you think about when you think about Louisville? If you're like most people who don't have a personal connection to the city, then you probably don't think of Louisville at all. I grew up in Cleveland, another Rust Belt city that most people don't think about, and like Louisville, when they do think about it, it's usually a caricature of the city's complexity.

In July 2009, my old red CRV rocketed down I-65 South to Louisville. In my mind I was speeding toward a certain image of Louisville. Horses.

Banjos. Whiskey. Racism. Homophobia. Xenophobia. Phobias. I packaged it into a tight little box that I created from scraps of what I saw on TV and heard in jokes.

Louisville is an amalgam of a cluster of regional identities. Midwest. South. Rust Belt. Farm Belt. Bible Belt. Union. Confederate. The city seems to have always straddled many lines, bearing the brunt of their converging fates.

The post-war economy is as close to its version of utopia as the United States has ever come and arguably ever will. That old postcard image of capitalism, of the American dream. The country had just asserted itself as a military superpower and industrial expansion in the Midwest founded the Steel Belt. GE built Appliance Park for its new Louisville headquarters and plant in 1951, shortly after International Harvester converted war plane factories into the main hub for heavy farm equipment manufacturing in the U.S.[1] Behemoth factories and mills permeated the countryside and new towns sprouted up around them.

American-made cars filled the streets and suburbs burgeoned in every pocket of the country. By 1960 the U.S. summited to the wealthiest nation in the world. At the same time, of course, the country was finally facing its reckoning with racial injustice, giving birth to the Civil Rights Movement in the early 1950s. The generous hand of the free market was discriminant in its giving and not everyone was a beneficiary of its bounty. The thing about utopias is that they aren't real.

A utopia is an unattainable ideal, as noble as the concept in question may be, in part because it implies permanence. It is a state where bliss meets eternity. When you're flying, it seems like you'll never land. When everything is up, it feels like it will never come down. That, however, negates time and nature.

Heavy manufacturing dropped in the late 1970s, which snowballed into a crisis. By 1982, the Steel Belt was officially the Rust Belt. For the first time in the twentieth century, Louisville's population shrank, losing almost a third of its residents from 1970 to 1990. The monumental highways built through Louisville in the 1950s[2], once a testament to progress, now teamed with Louisvillians pouring out of the city in search of opportunity.

As manufacturing ground to a halt, the farming crisis mushroomed. In the four short years from 1981 to 1985, a perfect storm of plummet-

1 | Cobb, James C. "The Sunbelt South." Essay. *In Industrialization and Southern Society,* 1877-1984, 53. *The University Press of Kentucky,* 2014.

2 | Jett, Richard, Joe Brent, Maria Campbell Brent, Tom Chaney, Sandra Wilson, and Dixie Hibbs. "Roadside Architecture of Kentucky's Dixie Highways." Field Session for Restore America: Communities At A Crossroads. Presented at the The 2004 National Trust for Historic Preservation Conference, October 1, 2004.

ing commodity prices and rising farm debt slashed land values across the Farm Belt.[3] The 1986 drought further smothered struggling farms and by 1987 farm values bottomed out.[4] Farmers abandoned their land and small farming towns collapsed like the manufacturing towns in the years prior. And in the center sat Louisville.

When I graduated college in Cleveland in 2009, the Rust Belt was in the throes of yet another economic calamity. Up and down, up and down. The most recent bust in the unceasing boom-bust wave inundated the news stream with the same old buzzwords. Interest rates. Bankruptcy. Foreclosure. Manufacturing. Unemployment. We woke up one day in late 2008 and everything we thought we built was revealed to be quixotic at best.

Louisville initially seemed to fit my idea of a sleepy Southern city. I visited Louisville for the first time to come to Forecastle Festival, which started as a small gathering in Tyler Park. By the time I attended Forecastle in the summer of 2009, the music festival had swelled to cover Waterfront Park.

I moved to Louisville the following month while most of my friends went straight into master's programs to ride out the 2008 recession, and the rest moved to big cities like San Francisco and New York City. I said that I chose Louisville because it was proudly weird and I wanted to do something different.

The truth was that I was desperate to get out of Cleveland where I grew up and stayed for college to appease my parents' demands. Are you even from the Rust Belt if you haven't feverishly dreamt of getting out of your hometown? The truth is that Louisville was the only place that I somewhat knew and could afford on my meager summer job savings. The truth was that I was looking for an escape.

Tension compounded for many people in 2009. The year started with the police shooting of Oscar Grant in Oakland. The economy was going through the worst recession since the Depression. In considering a bill that would have prevented same-sex couples from adopting, Kentucky was engaging in what many LGBTQI+ advocates deemed state-sponsored homophobia. We were walking tinder boxes and Marea lit the match.

Seemingly overnight, Louisville caught rave fever. Our DJ friends from Chicago drove in to play the parties and partygoers gathered from Lexington, Cincinnati, and St. Louis. The parties became more frequent and spread through the city. We took over art galleries, defunct restaurants,

3 | Tweeten, Luther. "Research Review: A Note on Explaining Farmland Prices in the Seventies and Eighties." *Journal of Agricultural Economics 38, no. 4* (1986): 25.

4 | Footnote text: Lawton, Kurt. "Taking a Look Back at the 1980s Farm Crisis and It's Impacts." *Farm Progress*, August 22, 2016.

bars, and the attics of Louisville's historic mansions-turned-apartments. Anywhere we could stuff three speakers and about a hundred guests.

———————

Dance music and the beginning of rave culture in America was kindled in the empty factories left in the Rust Belt's wake before spilling into rambling fields across the Midwest. As industry and farming left in the 1980s bust, the ravers moved in.

House music started on the heels of the dying commercial disco craze in the late 1970s. In 1977, Robert Williams started throwing dance parties in a Chicago warehouse, the eponymous Warehouse nightclub, where Frankie Knuckles played for many years.[5]

In the early 1980s, the AIDS epidemic gripped the most vulnerable American communities while society and our leadership stigmatized and abandoned them. By the time Reagan addressed AIDS in a speech for the first time in 1987, more than 20,000 Americans had already died.It seemed like the world was falling apart outside. But, at the risk of sounding melodramatic, inside Warehouse Frankie was saving their lives. When I was younger, I thought it was strange that music as upbeat and fun as jazz could be popular during the Great Depression. Now I understand it was beloved because it *was* the Depression.

The rave scene spread quickly through the Rust Belt because it was at once national and hyper-local. The parties were not driven by big celebrity names, which gave many new artists the opportunity to establish themselves without a record deal and cultivate a rabid following. For the first time for many people, they were finally in a place created just for them.

As raves spread through the Midwest, Louisville joined the party. The underground party scene was able to survive as long as it did because it was underground. It was a DIY scene that took over abandoned spaces, sometimes converting them to permanent nightclubs, and advertised on secret message boards for parties in undisclosed locations.

Local crew Evolution threw Teknosaurus parties that were promoted by flyers that often featured an ornery T-Rex smashing a record with its jaws. Louisville's cosmic Stardust parties featured DJs from Chicago that crisscrossed the Midwest with their record bags.[6] The Rust Belt rave scene in the 1990s was massive in part because revelers regularly traveled to neighboring cities. If the party was in Cincinnati, Louisville

5 | Arnold, Jacob. "The Warehouse: The Place House Music Got Its Name." Resident Advisor, May 16, 2012.

6 | "Louisville Flyer Gallery." Rave Preservation Project. Accessed July 12, 2020. http://www.ravepreservationproject.com/gallery/index.php#UnitedStates/Kentucky/Louisville.

would be drained of its dancers that weekend as they caravanned along the Ohio River.

Mainstream credit has largely gone to New York City and Los Angeles, of course. Michael Alig's Club Kids were synonymous with the New York club scene and large collectives like Global Underground Network proliferated through the West Coast.[7]

Dance music went mainstream in the late 1990s and it was the beginning of the end of the rave. NPR, *Dateline*, and other national news outlets had been reporting on the underground movement for several years at that point and to the nation-at-large the rave scene became synonymous with party drugs like ecstasy and ketamine. This attracted the attention of politicians and the police, along with the squatter nature of the parties.

The parties were more than just a drug binge, but there was definitely a drug element present and it is easy to see why. It's not fair to say that ravers did drugs just to have fun because the circus perpetually unfolding in front of them and driven by them and unrelenting bass was fun enough. The drugs added another layer of escapism that the scene already provided. Drugs were common because they served a similar and complementary purpose to the parties themselves. By the end, none of that seemed to matter.

Although I now worked to put on and run the parties in Louisville, I still felt like a tourist making my way through the smoke. In those dark warehouses and secret rooms, though, I did see who lives here. I saw the faces that I didn't associate with Louisville before, the ones most of the country overlooks, the identities I didn't consider. It wasn't white anymore. It wasn't cis or straight. Some were running away from something; others were looking for something. For a moment, they all heaved into rapture together, lost in a ceaseless rhythm. Up and down. Up and down.

The next year Marea moved back to Chicago. Her respite had come to an end and she was ready to create her future as The Black Madonna. And, once again, the party was over in Louisville.

As this anthology goes to print, we are all locked up in our homes. Outside, a pandemic rages on that keeps us apart as we lose our jobs and homes; as markets crash and food is taken from farms to landfills.

Something else is happening, too. The party is happening. The tradition born in Midwest warehouses and revived on internet message boards is taking a new shape. It's now in the glow of our screens, in the bass vibrating our windows.

No guestlist required.

7 | "A Little Rave History." Rave Preservation Project. Accessed July 12, 2020. http://www.ravepreservationproject.com/#history.

"Down Here": One View of Old Louisville

KIMBERLY GARTS CRUM

I am in queue at the Old Louisville Holiday Home Tour, when the woman behind me strikes up a conversation. "I wouldn't go out after dark if I lived *down here*," she says. "Just last week, my husband was *down here*. A man asked him for money . . . and he almost had a gun."

I have grown accustomed to peculiar statements by persons who visit historic Old Louisville. But this one is unique.

"Where do you think the people *down here* go to the grocery?" she says.

I've had enough. "Actually," I say. "I go to the Valu Market. . . . You might stop at my house down the street; it's on the tour, the Arts & Crafts home with the red tile roof."

"It looks like a wedding cake," my husband John had said, on a summer evening in 2006, when we first walked by the house on Saint James Court. He was referring to the three tiers of taupe stucco, plaster cartouche, and red tile roof.

We thought we'd forget the house; we were not planning a move. A month later, it was for sale by owner.

Prisms of light filtered through leaded glass windows. The rooms were a geometry of mahogany beams. On both glass and wood were motifs of oak leaves and acorns and gingko. The house was the new construction—circa 1911. Consequently, it lacked the "open concept" so popular among twenty-first-century HGTV hosts. No kitchen opened into a family room. No balcony overlooked the living room. It was all nooks and crannies, including what our daughters would refer to as the "Harry Potter" room under the stairs. We were smitten.

The next day, I found myself humming the tune from *My Fair Lady*, in which the lovesick Freddy croons about having walked down Eliza's street before, but the pavement had stayed beneath his feet before. In my view, a house that provoked a romantic melody deserved serious consideration. And so, we swapped our safe and predictable sixteen-year-old suburban home on a quiet cul-de-sac, for a drafty, creaky ninety-five-year home near the thumping heart of the city.

"I'm not moving," I announced one morning, certain we had made a terrible mistake. I was miles out of my comfort zone. My romance with the home had fizzled before the wedding. There would be costs, emotional and financial. We would be moving three animals and one seventeen-year-old daughter. We would pack the belongings of our older daughter, away at college. There were too many unknowns. Everything had happened so quickly. A sense of adventure prevailed.

I expected discomfort. I expected that my contemporary furniture would look odd in the old house. I expected arguments over paint colors. What I did not expect was to be surprised each day by things I had never seen before: a man walking two cats, one named Nelson Mandela and the other, Susan B. Anthony; another strolling the neighborhood on a Sunday morning, holding his poodles on a leash with one hand, and a Mimosa in the other; the alley-entrepreneurs pushing bascarts behind our garages; the man feeding Cheetos to the squirrels; homeless men napping on benches, shaded by hundred-year old trees and in the view of an 8,000-square-foot mansion. And there was the Osage orange tree in Central Park, gnarly and orange-hued, its bark a Rorschach of faces. A bear. An angry boy. A snake. I slide my fingers across the face of the bear and peer into portholes. I look away while a hawk in its branches dismembers a squirrel. The tree has become my talisman.

Old Louisville is a traditional place for nontraditional people. It is a wildly diverse community, haunted by two kinds of ghosts—wispy apparitions, and persons who famously (or infamously) lived and died in the spaces we now occupy. I had no previous acquaintance with the idea of haunted houses. Now, I believe in ghosts, or at least the vestiges of past lives. Sane people have ghosts in their homes; they hear footsteps, doors closing, the smell of cigars or perfume. "We tell the spirits how much we love the house," they say. "We smudge the house with a bit of sage."

I am most haunted by the stories of people who lived and died here: the Jewish merchants, industrialists, and philanthropists who built mansions on Millionaire's Row (aka South Third Street); the Women's Temperance Union (WCTU), which, in 1901, purchased the mansion now known as the Pink Palace. The story goes that the women discovered the mansion had been a gentleman's club, where men could drink, smoke, and gamble without female interference, the exception being a brothel on the third floor. As a protest, the WTCU painted the mansion pink, and so it remains.

I have never lived in a place so resonant with history. I love hearing tales of the artists, poets, potters, playwrights, and gay couples who bought distressed homes during the 1960s, effectively saving them. And there is the story of how a militant group of preservationists prevented an 1886 mansion on South Fourth Street from being razed for a parking lot, a few years after Joni Mitchell's popular song, "Big Yellow Taxi." Thus began the movement that made Old Louisville an historic preservation district.

Thirteen years after our move to Old Louisville, I continue to hear questions about what it's like to live *down here*. My elevator speech goes something like this—I love the architecture, the front porch culture, the moving landscape of bicycles and dog walkers, the proximity to downtown, the walkability, meeting people I know on the sidewalks, at the Burger Boy or Central Park. The Shakespeare Festival. Did you know there are owls in the park?

But some persons, like the woman who told me she'd never leave her house after dark if she lived *down here*, are more fearful than curious. Their questions refer to the presumed dangers of life in a dense urban setting.

A population of 10,500 lives in this 1.189 square miles area. Persons of all races and ethnic groups, ages, incomes, sexual orientations, and genders live shoulder-to-shoulder among forty-eight blocks of Victorian homes. There is poverty and wealth. There is crime and addiction. There are once-elegant homes abandoned or abused.

To people who still do not understand why I love living *down here*, I simply say, "I live with all God's children." Many of my neighbors have very little, which reminds me daily of my obligation to share my good fortune.

Of course, I often leave my house after dark.

Air Devil's Inn on a Saturday Night

BETH NEWBERRY

Air Devil's Inn is most alive on a summer night when the humidity is high, and the heat makes your clothes feel a little closer to your skin, a little heavier on your body. Air Devil's Inn, or ADI to the regulars, is the first bar I found when I moved to Louisville. My friend Ben introduced me to the bar with this endorsement: "I can get drunk on ten dollars and still have money for two games of pinball."

Claiming to be the oldest bar in Louisville, ADI is located across the road from Louisville's first airport, Bowman Field. The bar was a hangout for pilots on layover and it is their namesake. Flyers would cross the road for a couple of hours on the ground and grab a stiff bourbon or an Old Milwaukee. Those air devils are no longer regulars since a newer airport was built thirty years ago on the other side of town. The regulars changed from pilots to bikers, making the Inn a little bit of a rougher place, at least by reputation. While there are a couple of Harleys in the lot on any given night, the regulars now are a wide cross-section of white people—roots rock enthusiasts, divorcées on the make, and blue-collar workers getting off of second shift.

Inside the wooden door, on a weekend night, awaits a bouncer to collect a cover. The person working the door is never on the bar's payroll, but most likely a member of the band playing that night, a friend of the band, or even an ADI regular. The only requirement for working the door is the ability to drink, smoke and count money at the same time. Most nights it's Paul.

On this particular night, Paul works the door wearing a version of his uniform: cigarette, offensive t-shirt, jeans, white running shoes. His shirt reads, "Support local music, sleep with a musician." I make eye contact with him and think, "Oh, God, don't let him hit on me." Other t-shirts in his collection say things like "I Put Out on the First Date" and "Lord of the Cockring." Paul, in his late thirties, has the kind of tan that comes from a tanning bed. He looks almost orange. He sports a hairstyle he works hard to achieve. Part mullet with some Farah Fawcett-esque feathering on the sides. The final result is a Carol Brady-inspired coif. It gives a feminine edge to his otherwise burly physique.

"It'll be five bucks," he tells me. When he speaks, I hear the two-pack-a-day habit on his voice. It's not so much a haggard voice that smoking causes, but the deep corroding of the lungs that brings a constant cough with every light-up.

In the dim glow of the bar, model airplanes hang from the stained ceiling tiles. The support columns in the bar have old framed photos of pilots and newspaper articles about the bar from the '50s. It's a Saturday night at ten o'clock and members of that evening's band, Dallas Alice, stand around the bar with a few regulars and a few fans.

Alan and Gina work the bar most weekend nights. Alan always wears a red, laundry-faded Hawaiian shirt. He's in his forties, or maybe his fifties. Who can tell in the backlighting of a Bass Ale sign? He seems to have a kind spirit and is always friendly. When the bar is slower, usually on a week-night, he will quiz folks on politics or language trivia because he speaks five languages. Originally from Scotland, his accent has faded since he came to the U.S. in his teens. One night I was there and told him I was going to go home and write and he gave me pen and paper. "Only give it back to me after you write a good story on it," he said.

While Alan is efficient and kind in his service, Gina acts as if she would prefer no one come to the bar. If customers have to be there she would rather they speak to her as little as possible. I try to be pleasant and decisive and have cash ready when I go to the bar. She doesn't want to be messed with, and really she frightens me a little. A woman can wait fifteen minutes at the bar to order, no matter how empty the bar is in an evening. I don't even try to catch her eye as she's taking other orders down the bar. I lean in slightly and look interested in ordering, hold my money out to show I'm ready—there is no room for messing around. I wait patiently, trying not to appear anxious, put out or friendly. Nothing will get you ignored more quickly than actually trying to get her attention. As I wait, I practice my order in my head. She finally slows down as she walks by and points to my money.

"Bourbon and ginger ale, please," I say. She keeps walking and gathers beer bottles, filling the order of the man to my right who came to the bar after me. It doesn't matter who got there first, or how long I've been waiting, it's Gina's call. She comes back, a bit exasperated. It's more of a general statement about people coming to the bar than about me.

"What was it?" she asks again as she sets down four beers for the man in a North Face vest and polo shirt.

"Bourbon and ginger," I repeat. "A tall one," I add. I realize it's best to order a double, you know, planning ahead, because I don't know if I will be able to get another drink later on, depending on Gina's mood. She nods as the man tries to hand her a credit card.

"Oh, no. Cash only," she says as she points to the woman behind the customer who has taken her Rolling Rock. "Give me back that beer until you settle up." The man fumbles for enough cash, as he seems thrown by the rules of the dive: Cash only. No tabs. After he settles up, Gina hands me my drink, charging me fifty cents more than Alan would for the same drink, $3 instead of $2.50 which strikes me as criminal.

She shakes her head, "Don't hand me a credit card and think you can take your drinks," she says under her breath. I'm relieved to know enough to play by the rules. I drop two bucks—almost the price of the drink—into the tip jar in a quick gesture hoping she'll notice.

Gina has loose, blond curls with dark roots. She wears a wide, red bandana to keep her hair out of her face, and a sleeveless tee, perhaps a beach-vacation souvenir, over a visible sports bra. She tucks the shirt into her cut-off jean shorts that stop above her thighs. I think she wears such short shorts to show her muscular legs, not to garner high tips from the men at the bar, but as a quiet warning that she can kick your ass with her Reebok high tops if you get out of line.

I turn from the bar and look around. I see a couple of the guys from the band Dallas Alice at the end of the bar smoking and a couple on stage doing a sound check. I move to a bar stool at the end of the bar on the edge of the dance floor. Nick, the lead guitarist, is leaning against the bar drinking a bottle of Bud, smoking a cigarette. He arches his eyebrows and lifts his beer to gesture a hello. At forty-five, Nick is the oldest member of the band, while the other fellas are in their twenties or are right around thirty. He always wears a dark suit with a coordinating button-down shirt and bolero tie. He heads to the stage as I settle onto the stool. There are a few tables on the edge of the small dance floor, but since I came to ADI by myself I don't want to sit right in front of the band.

The five guys in Dallas Alice don't fancy themselves a band for bikers, truckers, or even the lonely old guy at the end of the bar. They see themselves as a bar band, or rather half-assed musicians that would be drinking at Air Devil's anyway so might as well get up on stage and sing some songs. Sean, the lead singer, has a voice that growls like a stick shift changing gears. The band's harmonies have an audible twang like empty beer cans rolling around in the bed of a pick-up. Sean writes most of the songs and his lyrics ride the line between country dirt roads and big-city blacktop. He's from southern Illinois, but he sings songs that could be about the small towns in eastern Kentucky where I grew up. The band's musical style could play in the background in some of the stories of my life, if I were to make them a movie. They weave together small town roots and the grown-up life of living in a city.

Sean has short blond hair he sweeps back in a miniature pompadour. He's wearing a short sleeved Steve Earle t-shirt that partially covers his tattoos. Most prominent is one on his forearm with his mother's name, Georgia, written across the shape of the state, fashioned like a vintage postcard with a peach in the foreground.

He sings the song "Free Coffee." He begins a cappella, *All the fields around my hometown grew milo beans and corn/ Now there ain't much but weeds and broken dreams/ That grows there anymore.* The rest of the band kicks in with a harmony, *It's just another small town. Small town slipping away.*

The drummer and the guitarists pick up and the stage comes to life. Patrons start to turn from the bar and edge toward the dance floor without actually stepping on to it.

Nick plays a hard-driving interlude on his Stratocaster. The younger guys he plays with cede the stage to him. His improvisational style lands somewhere between extended riffing and jamming. He moves the cigarette he is smoking to secure it under the guitar strings just above the neck of the guitar. A small crowd of eight or so people stands and watches attentively with drinks or cigarettes in hand. They sway to the music or bob their heads in time with the music.

I require a live band with enough Red Bull in its veins to help me paint the town a particular shade of roots rock red. I dig Dallas Alice because they can balance twang with tattoos, guitar solos with bourbon shots, and smart lyrics with foul mouths. The five members are slightly scruffy, occasionally charming, reliably boozy, and guaranteed to be smoke-stained. They serve their music neat, no mixers needed. After seeing them play on a few occasions, their music stole my honky-tonk heart. It has become a welcome soundtrack to my evening. I enjoy the people watching, the drinks, and the good company of friends always available at ADI. I answer the Dallas Alice altar call about once a month and I get doused in enough twang to keep me away from commercial country music until the next time I cross the threshold at ADI.

At the end of the first song, Gina delivers a tray of bourbon shots to the band. They each take one. Sean turns to the mic, as the applause slows. "We're Dallas Alice," he says raising the shot glass for a toast. "Social!" and the band's members knock their heads back and drink down the brown liquor. Regulars repeat Sean's call and tip back High Life bottles and glasses of whiskey. A table of young women in low-cut tank tops and tight jeans slam empty glasses on their table after finishing shots of Jägermeister.

People start to head to the dance floor. I leave my perch and move to a wall plastered with posters for upcoming shows. It's near the dance floor, but back far enough that I feel comfortable and slightly hidden. I watch the guitar playing and sing softly to myself.

Where Have All the Rolled Oysters Gone?

ASHLIE D. STEVENS

Rolled oysters are almost as integral a part of Louisville's drinking culture as bourbon, though with far less international fame. Italian immigrant Phillip Mazzoni began serving them in his eponymous nineteenth-century saloon as a humble bar snack—free to drinking patrons, like salted peanuts or pretzels. When patrons purchased a beer or a whiskey, Mazzoni would also slide them a plate of rolled oysters. Patrons developed a taste for them, which proved fortuitous. But while Louisville owes much to this unlikely local favorite, it's never quite received the recognition it deserves, making its slow but steady fade all the more poignant. In the twenty-first century, this oddball bar snack is rapidly tumbling off Louisville menus.

A rolled oyster is not, upon first inspection or bite, exactly recognizable as an oyster. Here's how they're made: take two or three small Chesapeake oysters, dip them in a milky egg wash and cornmeal batter called *pastinga*, and then coat in a thick cracker crust. Once deep-fried, they're about the size of a fist or a slightly flattened, misshapen softball, more coating than actual bivalve.

"Basically, you've encased this oyster in cracker meal [and] fried it. They burst and the inside of the morsel is just gooey goodness," Greg Haner, the last Mazzoni descendant to own the restaurant, told me. "Some people will say, 'There's no oyster in here!' but that just means that it's perfect."

When the Volstead Act took effect, establishing Prohibition across the United States, the ritzy Pendennis Club downtown was raided by federal agents who confiscated six carloads of bottles—gin, whiskey, and champagne. Production of tainted, homemade liquor surged; bars across the city shuttered. But Mazzoni's managed to stay open by charging for the rolled oysters they used to give away with drinks. As other bars-turned-restaurants around Louisville followed suit, rolled oysters became something of a local favorite, despite the fact that there's nothing particularly local about the main ingredient.

In a practical sense, the rolled oyster owes its life to transportation innovations like steamboats and railways, which allowed oysters to be shipped across the country from the East Coast. But as a cultural artifact it's also an enduring reminder that humans have a way of dealing with deprivation by trading one vice for another—in this case, swapping outlawed alcohol for the deep-fried delights of the bar snack, which at least carried memories of pre-Prohibition drinking days.

Rolled oysters are an acquired taste, Haner says, but one that kept Mazzoni's in business until 2008, when both the recession and surging oyster prices ultimately caused the restaurant to shutter. Turns out that was a harbinger of the rolled oyster fate, too.

In 2017, I ordered a shot of Old Forester and a basket of rolled oysters at The Silver Dollar, a Clifton whiskey bar, without even looking at the menu. This was my weekly vice, predictably indulgent. I was surprised to hear that that my regular order would have to change; rolled oysters were no longer being served.

"They were not priced out as well as they should have been," Erica Goins, the chef at Silver Dollar, told me at the time. "The pricing on the menu should have maybe been adjusted as our prices were increasing, but I think that they kind of wanted to keep them at the point they were to keep them available to people."

As the price of oysters continued to rise, Goins said, she struggled with charging entrée-level prices for the simple snack. "There was almost no profit margin," she said.

According to Don Webster, a regional aquaculture specialist with the University of Maryland extension, oyster prices have only risen over the last decade.

"In the Chesapeake and the mid-Atlantic, we had a couple of diseases that moved in that affected oysters," Webster said. "That dropped the harvest down now from what was about a 2.5 million bushel harvest—now we're about 10 percent of that."

It's that loss of supply that has driven the cost up. In the '70s and '80s, oysters cost $11 a bushel; in 2016, oysters hit $35 to $40 a bushel—which, when you factor in additional transportation costs and processing, explains why profits on the dish are dipping. While a diner might drop $2 on a raw oyster, the humble fried, rolled oyster doesn't command the same prices.

Webster was hopeful that increased conservation efforts and domestic aquaculture would help oyster prices plateau, which would bring Louisville's unique snack back to area bars—this time, for good. As the bourbon boom and Louisville's innovative culinary scene increasingly demand acclaim and outside attention, we shouldn't forget the unsung local heroes who have been served here all along, while we still remember how they taste.

Great Expectations in Louisville's Butchertown

FRED SCHLOEMER, WITH SUSAN E. LINDSEY

I first read Charles Dickens's *Great Expectations* in the eighth grade; it's a complex tale of ambition, hubris, and unrequited love. The story's characters include Pip, a young orphan; Miss Havisham, an eccentric spinster embittered by being stood up at the altar; and Miss Havisham's ward, Estella, a haughty young beauty. One of Dickens's most haunting images is of Miss Havisham's dining room table, frozen in time. There, she has left her uneaten bridal feast to rot—for decades. Spiders have festooned the candles with their webs, and mice have chewed holes in the desiccated wedding cake.

When I read this passage, I was immediately transported to an earlier time in my life, when another moldering dining room table captured my imagination—a table in Louisville's Butchertown neighborhood, a table I last saw more than sixty years ago.

Today Butchertown is a charming historic preservation district, where Federal-style townhouses hug the streets behind tiny front gardens and black wrought-iron fences. There is a European look and feel to the area, which makes sense, since it was built by immigrants, mainly German and Irish laborers and merchants. Colorful blossoms spill from window boxes, flowering vines sprawl over trellises, and some of the avenues are still paved with brick.

For many of the German immigrants, their strongest work skills were butchering and meat-processing. That's who my people were. My father's family had always been butchers and grocers, including our founding father, Karl Wilhelm Schloemer. My ancestors arrived in America and settled in Butchertown in the 1840s. Back then, most homes and factories burned coal, so the air and buildings would have been black with smoke and soot stains. Vehicles were drawn by horses or mules, and old photos of the area reveal streets littered with their droppings.

On his 1842 whirlwind reading tour through America, Charles Dickens reported that he loved Louisville, except for the fact that stray pigs roamed its streets, feeding on kitchen slops and making a frightful stench. Those pigs' citywide wanderings originated in Butchertown.

I grew up in another time and in a different Louisville neighborhood, St. Matthews, only a few miles away from Butchertown, but a world away culturally. It was the 1950s, during the post-war new home construction boom. We lived in a white-frame Cape Cod cottage on a street lined with lawns, sapling shade trees, and lots of homes exactly like ours.

I always knew that our roots were in Butchertown, though. We often visited elderly relatives there who reminded us of our history. They shared their memories of the days when Butchertown was a gritty, malodorous business district and working-class enclave. By the 1950s, it had fewer meatpacking plants than it once had. Nevertheless, the air still reeked with the pungent smells of blood, manure, and urine from its stockyards, and sewage from the polluted waters of nearby Beargrass Creek. All of these were juxtaposed with the sweet, savory scent of hams and sausages curing in the neighborhood smokehouses.

From its founding in the 1820s until World War II, most Butchertown residents owned shops in the area or worked in one of the slaughterhouses or meat-packing plants that were its biggest employers. These residents usually built modest houses, short on frills and highly utilitarian, frequently above or behind the businesses they operated.

One exception was the home of my Aunt Lorena and Uncle Fred Schloemer, widely known as the Layer mansion. It was one of the largest, and at one time, most elegant homes in Butchertown, although it, too, had a shop and packing plant behind it.

In its day, the house was considered one of the nation's foremost examples of the Victorian Rococo style. The house was extravagantly decorated, inside and out, with ornately carved woodwork, stained glass windows, and marble or wood sculptures of smiling angels, snarling gargoyles, and gazing stag heads. As a child—younger than Pip—I roamed its labyrinthine hallways and found it as fascinating as it was spooky.

Part of my fascination with the house derived from the quirky family story of how it came to be built in the first place. It was built by my grandfather Karl's best friend and business associate, Gottlieb Layer, a portly, cigar-chewing, larger-than-life character. Gottlieb was brusque, tremendously ambitious, hard-working, and very rich, and one of the so-called "big boss butchers." He didn't trust American banks and had stashed his ample fortune in various hiding places throughout his house. Eventually, his wife prevailed upon him to deposit his money somewhere other than under the floorboards. She feared being robbed and murdered over it more than Gottlieb feared banking it.

Reluctantly, he turned his money over to the nearby Stockyards Bank. Almost immediately, he regretted the decision and went to the bank to retrieve it; however, the manager talked him out of it. Time and again, he tried to withdraw his funds, but each time the persuasive banker changed his mind.

Finally, Gottlieb came up with an unusual solution. He resolved to build a new house in front of the business he owned at the corner of Story Avenue. Bragging to friends about his clever plan, Gottlieb revealed he would pay for the building with a long series of checks. The slick-tongued bank manager would never know his money was trickling out of the bank until it was gone.

Gottlieb soon realized that in order to get all of his considerable fortune out of the bank, he was going to have to build a very large, very extravagant house. Never one to be daunted by an arduous task, in 1889, he set to work building, making most of the decisions about the home's ornate design and adornments himself. The fruit of his labor was the grandiose Layer mansion.

My Uncle Fred married Lorena, Gottlieb's eldest daughter. She inherited the house with the stipulation that she would care for her younger, somewhat simple sister, Amelia, as long as they both lived.

By the time I saw the mansion, it was definitely a faded beauty. I never saw the entire house, but I know that it had dozens of rooms throughout its three stories, connected by several large hallways and staircases. The first floor had twelve-foot ceilings with thick crown molding; a vast central entry hall that ended in a massive, winding walnut stairway; two front parlors—one for formal entertaining and another for informal events; a library; and a huge dining room connected by a butler's pantry to a combination breakfast nook and kitchen. Huge trees shaded the house and a weed-infested formal garden. Stretching tree limbs encroached on the house, making it dark and cold inside and causing moss to grow on its exterior walls.

The floors were a pale oak parquet inlaid with darker hardwood mosaic designs. In most of the rooms and hallways, threadbare Persian rugs and runners covered the floors. They were probably worth a fortune.

The tall doors and windows featured stained glass geometric designs and various mythological characters and events. Inside, the woodwork was carved black walnut, made even darker by the mahogany stain ubiquitous in Victorian times.

The walls were papered with flocked wallpaper in different muted hues of red, gold, and green. Around some of the fireplaces and windows, the wallpaper was cracked and peeling.

Most of the furniture was massive and dark. The sofas and easy chairs were covered in scratchy horsehair, their wood backs, arms, and legs carved into rosebuds and bird claws.

Everywhere there was some eye-catching and often mystifying sight. My aunts and uncle loved Christmas, so they kept a heavily decorated Christmas tree in every room, which they lit every night, all year round. An old photo of the home's façade shows Christmas wreaths hanging on all the windows.

They also were avid readers, and almost every surface held a stack of books, newspapers, and magazines. The house had a musty scent of old paper mingled with smoke from the cigars my uncle always wedged in the corner of his mouth and the cigarettes the ladies smoked all day.

By far, the most jaw-dropping sight in the house was the long, seemingly endless dining room table—the table I had thought of when I read Dickens's description of moldering wedding cake. The dining room set was made of deep red mahogany and a dozen heavy, brocade-upholstered chairs surrounded the table. Overhead, a wide crystal chandelier lit up the room like a night ballgame, even though many of its bulbs were burned out or missing. There was also a large, floor-model radio, and I never visited the house that it wasn't on at a low volume. "To keep us company," Amelia said.

I also never visited that I didn't find the three of them gathered closely together around one end of the big table, all reading something or other, and chatting amiably. They all seemed terribly old to me, but I know now that they were younger then than I am today.

Amelia was a short, plump woman with long gray hair that she wore in a girlish ponytail. She spoke like a little girl, as well, rattling on nonstop, whether anyone was listening or not. As lost in the past as Miss Havisham, Amelia loved talking about the numerous rich, handsome suitors she had had as a young debutante. She had never married, though, no matter how many beaux she might have had. She always wore a faded silk housedress and a number of antique rings flashed on her hands as she chattered.

While dismissing most of her stories as prattle, my father admitted she had indeed been very beautiful as a young woman, but she had also "never been right in the head."

Lorena and Fred were extremely thin, with snow-white hair; hers piled high in a bun on the top of her head and his in a short military cut. Both also had bright blue eyes that twinkled when they spoke and pink cheeks that conveyed a sense of vitality despite their infirmities.

Though her face was lined and wrinkled then, it was clear from her beautiful bone structure and self-assured carriage that Lorena had once been a very handsome and much-admired woman. She always wore a black, high-collared silk dress and a white lace shawl over her shoulders.

Fred was unassuming and came across more as "a regular Joe." From the way he gazed at his wife, it was obvious he still adored her and couldn't quite believe he'd ever been lucky enough to win her hand. He wore flannel shirts, corduroy dungarees, and a tweed English driver's cap, even inside the house.

Aunt Lorena had been disabled years before in an accident of some kind that no one ever discussed; it was referred to obliquely in whispers as "the incident." She always used an old-fashioned, high-backed wooden wheelchair, and she slept on a daybed inside the bay window in the library.

Since they all smoked, the room was always filled with a thick, blue-gray pall. In addition, every room on the first floor had a shallow coal-burning fireplace. They were often cold, so a smoldering coal fire burned in every grate much of the year. Sometimes the air was close to suffocating.

However, what made the biggest impression in the dining room was the amazing array of clutter on the long, lace-covered table. Rising above the chaos, several tall candelabras of tarnished silver stood sentinel. Piled on the table beneath them, stacks of books and periodicals gathered dust. Ashtrays overflowed, dirty dishes attracted flies, open boxes of mixed chocolates spilled empty wrappers, and big cut-crystal bowls of multicolored hard candies sparkled. The candies were usually stuck together from the oppressive heat.

Once I asked my parents why my aunt and uncle's house was so unkempt. They explained that they were used to having help but could no longer afford servants and were too old and frail to do much for themselves.

Despite their reduced circumstances, the three of them always welcomed us warmly: my parents, me, and my siblings Marion and John. They had no children of their own and few visitors of any kind, so they seemed to relish having children in the house.

We visited these gracious elders weekly from the time of my earliest memories. The protocol was always the same. We would all chat together a bit until we kids got bored and stole away on our own. As we drifted from room to room, ogling the various treasures and oddities, we would catch pieces of the adults' ongoing conversation, mainly an exchange of news about who among their acquaintances was sick, who was in the hospital, or who had died recently.

Lorena, Fred, and Amelia had a knack for making each of us feel special, one way or another. Whatever we said, no matter how inane it might have actually been, they would ooh and aah over us until we became quite full of ourselves. They always invited us to take whatever sweets we wanted, then roam about the sprawling house. We usually took them up on both invitations, although none of us ever rallied the courage to venture up the deeply shadowed stairway—that was a bridge too far.

Uncle Fred suffered from what he called "rheumatiz" and had retired from working in the butcher shop, which continued to do a good business behind the house. He was still part-owner, though, so my father would ask him what items were good that day at the shop, and Uncle Fred would tell him what to purchase. I wouldn't realize until years later when it was no longer available to us, that my family once enjoyed truly exceptional meat at a huge bargain, far better than what was available at our neighborhood Piggly Wiggly.

Finally, my favorite part of these visits would come—a trip to the butcher shop. From out front, the shop looked shabby and uninteresting, but as soon as we walked through the door, we would be awash in a flood of glorious sights, sounds, and smells. If I close my eyes and turn back time, I can still hear the little bell that tinkled over the door and smell the clean cedar sawdust the butchers spread on the wood floors each morning.

Inside the spotless glass display case, a cornucopia of tantalizing meats and cheeses tempted buyers to overindulge—big loops of bratwurst and fat garlic frankfurters, various hard and soft sausages and salamis, thick slabs of beef and pork, and cheeses of all types, textures, and smells, some so potent they made us hold our noses. The air was redolent with the scent of hams, both smoked and sugar cured, and the herbs that had been mixed into different sausages and cold cuts—fennel and sage being most prominent.

Behind the case, several large, mustachioed, cigar-smoking men—who still spoke German to each other—would put on a show for us. Filling customers' orders, they would deftly weave around each other, and despite their big bellies, they somehow managed to avoid disemboweling one another with their menacing-looking knives and cleavers.

As they wove about, they'd bellow out questions to customers.

"How thick do you want these cutlets, ma'am?"

"You want a hunk of this nice, fresh salami, sir?"

Then they would make a startling noise whacking the meat on the cutting board, bringing the cleaver down so hard that the floor would shake. Whenever the noise made some timid soul jump nervously, the men would roar with laughter.

"That was some good whuppin', *ja?*"

They wore long white aprons spattered with blood and cigar ash. I sometimes wonder how much cigar ash found its way into our sausage and hamburger.

Sometimes, one of them would invite us kids into the cooler to help take down one of the sides of beef or pork hanging from sharp hooks overhead.

"I need me a big strong boy," the butcher would say. "Are you a big strong boy?"

I would nod an enthusiastic yes, even though I knew I was small for my age. The butcher would squeeze my bicep, feign an appreciative gasp at how big it was, and off we'd go to the cooler, one of his big, muscled arms around my shoulders.

Even though I knew we were both pretending, I always felt privileged and important on those occasions. If a health inspector had seen children inside the cooler, the butchers probably would have faced a hefty fine.

Our visits to the mansion ended when the relatives died, one after the other, in very short order. Aunt Lorena died in 1962 of a sudden, massive stroke. I was twelve, and her viewing was the first time I had ever seen a dead person. I had to struggle to keep from fainting. Only a few months later, Uncle Fred followed her, also of a stroke, although he lingered in a coma for several weeks. Amelia was too mentally challenged to live alone, so she was admitted to a nursing home where she, too, soon died.

The big house now felt cavernous and melancholy. My father and his two older brothers were the only heirs, but the brothers lived far away. All three of them were too busy with their families and careers to take on the responsibility of renovating or selling the house.

They hired an estate auctioneer, and in 1965, the house, butcher shop, and land sold at auction for a mere $4,000. The purchaser was a salvage firm that demolished the buildings, then resold the land at a huge profit as prime commercial property. There have been successful businesses of various types on the site ever since.

Today, it's almost inconceivable—for young people especially—that, not so long ago, people did most of their shopping in their own neighborhood. Usually this shopping was as much a social event as it was a necessary household chore. Merchants were family friends who exchanged news, gossip, and jokes with their customers. They made special orders and set aside treats for favorite customers. They made people feel important, and in my case, even loved.

To the best of my knowledge, Aunt Lorena and Uncle Fred's store was the last small family-owned butcher shop in Butchertown. I'm very proud and grateful to have been part of a family that provided such warm, high-quality services and goods for their friends, family, and neighbors. Amazingly, they did this for more than 120 years. I'm even more proud and grateful to have the treasure chest of memories that I do.

The sale of their estate should have been the end of the Layer mansion story for me, but it wasn't. Seven years later, in my sophomore year as a liberal arts major at the University of Louisville, I took a number of art history classes. One was a course on Louisville's outstanding residential architecture.

One day I was daydreaming during a long slide show, when I heard the instructor say something about the Layer mansion. Snapping to attention, I looked up to see a slide of the old house's impressive façade, a black-and-white photo taken in the house's glory days. At the sight of it, I felt a rush of intense nostalgia, a bittersweet blend of happy memories and sadness.

I heard the instructor describe the house as "a masterpiece of the Rococo Period in Victorian architecture." I'd never heard the term, but still felt a surge of pride that it had once belonged to my family.

Then I cringed and wanted to slip out of sight when the instructor added, "Tragically, the house was razed shortly after its owners' deaths, by numbskull heirs who didn't know what a gem it was."

I mused as I walked to my car after class. My instructor had been right about one thing; we hadn't realized that the Layer mansion was an architectural jewel. Although my parents were well-educated, even cultured people, they didn't travel in architectural circles. In addition, the condition of the house had deteriorated so badly few people would have considered it worth anything at all.

My instructor had been wrong about another thing; for me, at least, the old house had indeed been a gem. Some of my great expectations about life and how to live it well had been nurtured within its lichened walls. I learned about the value of things that may at first appear old, worn-out, or useless, but still have beauty and worth. I realized the importance of knowing one's family history, fables, and lore, and the blessings that can be found through exploring these with each other. Finally, I gained a real understanding of the inexorable nature of time and change, which make it incumbent on all of us to cherish the now.

The Shop

ASHLEÉ CLARK

"Used to be" is the language of Dixie Highway and the people for whom this street is the lifeline out. The trampoline park used to be Bacon's, where my twentysomething parents met as hairdressers in the department store's salon. The Kroger used to be Kmart, where my mother took me to get a red Icee and ride on the mechanical horse outside. The Hobby Lobby used to be Dixie Dozen, the movie theater where I had my first date with the boy who would become the man I married.

On and on down Dixie, I see the life I used to have before I left Shively, the child I used to be. But tucked away on Rockford Lane, one of the streets that flows south off the highway, is my "always been": J.T.'s New Attitude Beauty Salon. My dad is J.T., John Thomas, the owner and proprietor. My mother, Gayle, is his right-hand woman, the neck that makes sure the head of the business moves in the right direction. They do hair alongside three other women. My parents have been in this space for twenty-seven years, the majority of my life.

It's not much to look at when you pull into the parking lot. The salon sits in a runt of a strip mall with four other storefronts. On the far left is a convenience store/gas station with no gas; the overhang, where the pumps used to be, provides a convenient place to hide your car from the sun. To the right is an abandoned barbershop with a sign still in the window. Next to that is another empty storefront; there aren't any blinds over the windows, so you can see straight inside to an abandoned worksite—there are still sawhorses and a Styrofoam sixty-four-ounce cup longing for its owner to return. At the end of the strip on the far right is a closed soul food restaurant that used to be a bar. Between the worksite and restaurant rests J.T.'s New Attitude Beauty Salon.

It's the Shop to everyone who passes through the glass door. To me, it's a time machine. My parents have left the décor pretty much the same as it was when they moved into this building in 1992. The walls at some point looked like raspberry sorbet but have matured into mauve after almost thirty years of catching hairspray and spritz. Gold-framed pictures of generic African women hang in the back room with the shampoo bowls and the dryers. Tired duct tape holds together gaps in the cream styling chairs in the front of the Shop. Push pins and thumb tacks hold product posters onto the walls, artifacts from when brands like Affirm and Revlon pushed their chemical relaxers by featuring beautiful Black models with bone-straight long hair.

When I step inside the Shop, I am not a woman or a wife or a working professional. I am Gayle and John's daughter, the girl I used to be. The pictures they've each slid into the frames of their mirrors trace my childhood and transition to adulthood but stop just short of where I am now. Every time their ladies look at their hair, they see me on the periphery of their reflections. I am four in a dress with the colorful buttons with my chin on my hands, my eyes glancing away from the camera, an apprehensive grin on my face. I am fourteen, in a floor-length navy gown with "1999" written in rhinestones on the bust, my first formal dance at my first sleepaway camp. I am eighteen, home from my first semester of college, in front of a homemade backdrop wearing my favorite turquoise Old Navy top. I am twenty-three, with my boyfriend and my teenage nephew, our faces dark and dewy after a day at Holiday World.

My parents' customers, whom they call their "Ladies," kept up with me through those pictures. I didn't think about the Ladies much when I was a kid. They were just characters in the stories my parents told when they got home. Many of the Ladies had been with my parents since the Shop's beginnings, so their names and the rules for addressing them were clear from an early age. Grandma-age women were always "Miss" and their last name. Women my mother's age were always "Miss" and their first name. Miss Tillman, Miss Barbara, Miss Donna, Miss Salsbury. A first name by itself was too naked and familiar for addressing an elder in the Shop's universe. The Ladies were also, in a very technical way, my benefactors. They paid for my parents' services, so my parents could pay for my life. The photos on the mirror were like updates to what their money had done—travel, education, a comfortable life.

Yet the Ladies' relationships with my parents were more intimate than just client and service provider. I listened to my parents recount the drama their Ladies would confide in them: man troubles, kid troubles, troubles just being a Black woman in a world not designed to see them thrive. They probably didn't mean to, but these stories showed me how hard it would be to be Black and be a woman, to live at the intersection of weariness and heartache, to be the heart of a community that police, government, and regular citizens seemed all too eager to shoot down, soul by soul.

Most of the Ladies rolled into the shop at least once every other week, more often if paychecks allowed and nappy roots demanded. They submitted as soon as my parents flung a vinyl cap around their shoulders. Imagine another person's fingertips rubbing away dirt from you scalp, their hands applying a pressure that you didn't know you ached for, whose fingertips scratch the scalp and make you feel relieved and pampered. Imagine the trust it takes for you to close your eyes while another person looms over you like a chandelier from a short ceiling, their hands close enough for their watches and bracelets to graze your ears. Imagine the rubbing, the scratching, the relief of the water washing away week-old hair product and spent shampoo suds, the comfort of a dry towel around your head.

I didn't understand the intimacy until I became a Shop regular. This happened around the same time that my pictures did an inverse Dorian Gray and stopped aging at my parents' stations. They stopped hanging pictures when I moved back to Louisville. I had been away from home for seven years for college and my first job, a failed foray into the newspaper journalism career for which I thought I was destined. When I came back, my mother made me a standing appointment: 9:30 a.m. every Saturday, a coveted slot on a Black woman's calendar. Maybe my parents didn't need new pictures because they had something better—the person whom they raised in the business that they built, someone they could reach out and touch every week, not frozen in a moment, but fluid in the present. The Ladies became real. Miss Tillman came in on Saturday mornings at 10:30 so my dad could roller-wrap her gray hair. Miss Barbara dished about all the new adventures her boyfriend, Bill, whisked her off to. Miss Donna, a fellow coffee drinker, called me "Darlin'" and carried a plastic purse covered in Michelle Obama pictures. Miss Salsbury often brought her husband and recounted what she bought on her latest shopping trips. Every week, these women went from black-and-white to technicolor as I watched from a chair with duct tape that stuck to the backs of my thighs.

I've put some distance between myself and the Shop in the last few weeks. My schedule has been busy; there's always something I have to do on a Saturday morning. But sometimes, the only thing I want to do is sleep in. But I miss that storefront that has become my home. I miss my second cousin Grace hollering over the drone of her dryer to gossip with my mom. I miss hearing my dad walking in with his "How you doing there, ladies?" And his "Hey, pooka wooka" when he spots me during my deep conditioning. I miss the alarm that rattles my ears for a few seconds too long every time someone opens the door. I miss the sounds—the gospel from Gwen's room, the sizzle of frying pans on the Food Network that's always playing on the TV in the corner, the soft whoosh of my mom's desk fan she made me order online, the spray of the nozzle and the clunk it makes when my parents let it drop into the black bowls so they can use both hands to shampoo. The whirring of blow dryers to knock out that extra bounce that made a roller wrap just a little too curly.

As a grown woman, I need the Shop. I need this place to remind me not of who I used to be, but the person that I've always been: John and Gayle's daughter.

4/8/18:
From Lytle Street to Syria

CALEB BROOKS

In an old neighborhood
in a riverbend
in the greatest nation on Earth
a boy picks through a junk day pile set out a week early.
Comes away with a stroller, pair of baby shoes,
the aluminum flower of a rusted exhaust fan.

In Douma children lay on rugs foaming at the mouth
as the sarin turns the magnificent nervous system
of each on itself. (Neurotransmitter just being another
made-up word for miracle.) The lavish eyelashes of babies
flutter while the wailing rises, epochal.
The children lay on piles of blankets in dark corridors
and do not look dead until one is lifted and
the body is rigid like a thing frozen in bloom.

(The hollow we feel is empire: the violence of decay
here connected to war there by impulses of
greed and longing that destroy by ignorance
anything deemed unsacred.)

I do nothing but watch as the boy places the shoes
and scrap metal in the stroller and moves down the block.
A robin bathes with something like vigor
in a puddle of melted April snow that, once still,
mirrors the dendrite cupola of bare elms
flickering with the first evidence of spring.

Maybe I will find time to mourn and maybe not.
The mulch needs to be shoveled from the truckbed
before dark and there's ever the question of dinner
and anyway sorrow has no beginning, or end, or middle.

Et in Arcadia Ego

DAVE HARRITY

We lived in a house on Lee Avenue in Camp Taylor when we moved to Louisville. A blue-collar neighborhood of Cape Cods & bungalows, the mingling of kempt & unkempt yards, chain link & broken sidewalks, hilly with oaks & cathedrals & post-war predilection.

Across our street—a city park & pool. A good place for children to grow up seeing the varieties of lived experience: from stay-at-home moms to leather tramps camping for a night behind the cinderblock lav. Up the street, Lolita's Taco (all the perverse connotation implied) & Marmaduke's, where bikers, bitches, & third-shifters would sip beer, carouse, & shout at summer softball any hour of the day. Sometimes a brawl, but only late at night, & only in the lilted swell of dead-summer, when the air thickens around cicada trilling—heat & noise cross-stitching into a palpable, living ache—a brink, a rash blistering for reaction.

For the most part, it's a keen & quiet neighborhood—folks walking streets named for presidents, generals, & other American heroes of our burning wars stateside & abroad. The area boomed after World War I, when the land, which was a military installation, was decommissioned & developed for residents. The barracks became apartments—most of the standing houses there today built with wood repurposed from the base. The only obvious remnants that this land was anything else entirely: a small cemetery in a neighbor's back yard & a Naturalization Monument in Zachary Taylor Park, commemorating immigrants swearing oaths to fight for the United States. Hard to imagine it was once the country's largest training camp, &—before that—rolling farms of cotton, corn, & canola. How everything was something else & is becoming something else at every moment—and me trying to mark distinctions, variance.

Once, digging up his yard for massive daffodil beds, Chris found gnarled fragments of an artillery shell. The past was never far from him. He showed our children, doe-eyed Irish twins under four years old, the mortars. They were immediately taken with Chris who seemed to understand their innate curiosity. He paid attention to them.

Chris exchanged his drugs and drink for other addictions years before we met him: pouring concrete, praying to Mary, & expanding his yard into a strange garth of small ponds, gaudy sculptures, a hen house, & any variety of flowering vegetable that would flourish. Frenetic, he never hid his moods, but he was never anything but kind, however withdrawn or grumpy, to us & our kids. When we needed a banister in the stone stairs of our house, he put one in & didn't charge us a dime. When our water heater exploded the first week in the house, he gave us his keys so we could have a hot shower.

The year we moved, I taught English courses, trying to get students to understand that they have choice, autonomy. That writing is a declaration of agency—a comma or a contraction are decisions. That a sentence isn't just a mode of communicating but a way to raise your hand up in the world & say what you are, want to be. A decade later, I still believe this, but I've adjusted my expectations for their revelations.

I would see Chris here & there and he would ask me questions about what I thought about God. I could never explain my belief to him. He thought I was a doubter & said so once, not meanly, necessarily, but frankly & with the surprise and frustration of a convert. It's not that I don't believe, but that the only god I understand is a conversation between two people, the sun glinting off a bat across the park, the night noise of laughter at the bar, or the way a stranger smiles when they give you help you wouldn't ask for, like tossing you the keys to their front door. Yes, Chris, I pray sometimes. Yes, Chris, I know about Jesus. Yes, Chris, I know you're telling me so that I won't spend eternity in fire and pain. Yes, I know you're worried about the children, too. It's hard to fault the intentions of a man who lost & rebuilt his life on the back of dying 100 times over, whose only reason of living is the work he does daily to suppress his addiction.

He'd jokingly call me Thomas on occasion. I was unbothered by it, holding back my opinion: Thomas was the only apostle who made any sense to me. The impulse to feel & express physical inclination, to ask for touching. Apostles could chastise all they want, call into question another's faith—whatever. Curiosity can be mistaken as incredulity if you insist on putting your fingers in a wound.

The first spring in that house: I pull into our driveway next to Chris's yard & a thousand daffodils in full bloom. They were green when I left to grade papers early that morning in the blue dawn, the neighborhood asleep. By the late afternoon they are wild & bright & unafraid. Each year after that, they bloomed two weeks after my wife's birthday. An earthen liturgy worthy of veneration. I have never hoped to be saintly, but the perfection of nature helps me dream such things for myself—nature's divine & consistent resolve, easily recognized as holiness. Four springs passed, the children grew a bit & we didn't understand how fast the world was moving, was predictable. Each spring, with their fidelity to life and death, the flowers appeared & we remembered they were there all over again, surprised by the simplicity of things working as they should.

Some mornings, I wake up & am astonished by my luck. I am breathing, bleary-eyed—that my life is my life. The body cleaned & whole again. Not every morning, just many of them. The world is a tuning fork humming out another day, clean & bright. I kept at work—grading papers, making poems. I spent many mornings & nights rearranging sentences, trying to keep my hand up, trying to touch the moon on either side of the day.

The consequence of my tenuous faithfulness against someone who easily believes. My only core belief: I must enter God if I am to keep believing. I want the opening & the mettle gathered up in my fingers, I want the unsentimental gore of the body. Where can I put them in, O my bloodied Christ? Is doubter the cruelest superlative that the believer can manage against the bold?

Another birthday for my wife & this year it falls on Easter. A day to celebrate dead things coming to life on a day to celebrate her life. We come home to find our neighbor Chris dead in his driveway, a pistol slacked in his hand, the side of his head broken like a melon rind. A stillness I had never seen before.

You fool, do not make a mistake: You must be brave after asking. You wanted to live & recognize you were living, you wanted flesh & blood & refused to believe in resurrection. Today has become the day. Did you forget that Thomas asked & Christ said yes?

The stillness in the driveway. What comes next is only fragments, images of a day's passing & the significance of a life gone as quickly as a spring downpour. You will never get the details exactly, never be able to name it quite correctly.

First was the phone call. Then a duration—maybe twenty minutes? Maybe thirty? I sat with the body. Sat next to it, watched his blood soak into the gravel, watched a fly who found him. Careless flitting, jagged motion on his hair, the blue-lipped circumference of—no, did you look at his face? Yes, the wince. One eye pointed down & the other precisely taut, his jaw slack & salmon. His jeans, his red shirt, his jean jacket. The pistol limp in his hand, the gun & its one goddamn talent: to tear through & sleep until called to make another ending.

The police. Then neighbors. Then family. It was Easter; they were all together. He had not come to lunch, he had not gone to church. The sun & blue of the sky against the green of the park's glade. The crowd was growing as the yellow tape belted about in the wind. Then the priest & his immediacy, his panting panic ducking under the line & running to the stillness. If he did not get to the body in time, Chris would not make it to Heaven. But Hell was so close & so present that anything that could move seemed like love & charity.

I had found the stillness. I could walk between them—between the stillness & the family, past the police line. Strange ferryman, unprepared shepherd. I found the only rosary I owned & gave it to Chris's father. They were rapt, speechless, exhausted by daylight. When they were allowed to cross the line, the eldest brother went ahead. No other family could find the path forward. The brother walked past the stillness & up the stairs to the front door, reported that the house had been cleaned, that there were arrangements neatly laid out on the kitchen counter—everything was in order.

Here is where you must enter. Give me your hand. Which fingers would you like inside me? Which piece of you will become a piece of me?

The police were packing up, swaddling the stillness into a black bag without ceremony. I ask about what they will do with the pieces of him that are no longer part of him, the gray matter, the slit of skull, the jellied clots caked onto snatches of rock and plant. *We don't clean that up,* they say. Neither do any of us.

What their faces must have looked like when the doubter kept reaching in. It must have been the first time any of them—any of them—felt awe, knew belief. Thomas with his limp-dicked moxie now nauseous with flesh; the others with their self-righteous sycophancy twilled with desire to touch. *How do you want me now?* says Christ.

The whole foundation of the world trembles with the confluence of what we say & never have to act on, of the dumbfounded, striding arrogance to ask questions from a place of privilege—all the strawmen, all clean fingernails that go into shutting everyone the fuck up. What lies I tell myself about my goodness or my foolishness?

And that is today. I must clean up the brain of a man that I knew. No one will ask, but his mother shouldn't have to see the body that she grew inside her laid across a lawn like elements on a dinner table. I find a shovel, a bucket, & set to scooping up the parts of my neighbor to bury in a hole I will dig in his garden.

After that, the putting to rest of the dead. The funeral in the rain, Chris's fellow church go-ers far off & praying because Chris was the kind of Catholic where rules about suicide still mattered more than anything else & they couldn't mourn next to his body. The members of his congregation crying on their own, with their priest, for a soul that is forever damned. The family, also Catholic, just wanting to bury a boy who lost his way without fear that some fleshless God might remember their sins. Why do any of us believe this shit?

For weeks, I am the person who found Chris. For weeks, people walk by the house and talk to me—ex-girlfriends, a nun, old drinking buddies, cousins. It seems I moved into this house for one reason: to help him die or to help the living unpack his dying.

People light candles & place them on the gravel. People cry in front of me. I sit on the dark porch each night & try to record all of it—what I feel, what I think, what I wish might be different. None of it matters to anyone, or even to me anymore.

I will say this, & I don't blame you if you doubt me, as I was the one who didn't know what he was asking when Chris asked if I had any faith at all:

in April, in May, in June— into the summer—the daffodils Chris planted greened, but not a single one flowered. Not one.

God and Tennis

NORMAN "BUZZ" MINNICK

He asked if he could share the bench
with me. His name is David Crawford
and he wanted to know what I was reading.
William Blake. Poetry. Do you get into
spiritual things, he asked. Sure, I replied,
still not seeing what was coming.
Do you mind if I share my beliefs with you,
and he continued with the usual—finding salvation
through Jesus Christ, the Bible as God's word,
and so on. I had looked hard
for a bench in a secluded area
with no luck and settled on this one
alongside the walking path
in the busiest section of the park. As he talked
I watched two teenage girls play tennis.
I asked him who he thought was better,
Venus or Serena Williams. He said
he doesn't follow tennis. He said he is a student
at The Southern Baptist Theological Seminary.
I asked who he thought God was talking to
when He said, "Let us make man
in our image." The thock, thock from the tennis court.
The laughter of children from the playground,
the squeal of a swing set.
He said it was Jesus and the Holy Spirit.
He wanted to talk about atonement.
I tried to engage him in a conversation
about metaphor when a tennis ball landed at his feet.
He looked at it as if he had never seen a tennis ball before
then chucked it back over the high fence.

"Remain Silent": One Woman's Experience in Louisville's Baptist Churches

OLGA-MARIA CRUZ

When I arrived in Louisville in January of 1995, as a new student at The Southern Baptist Theological Seminary (SBTS) in St. Matthews, one of my top priorities was to find a new "church home." Most seminarians had jobs serving or pastoring a church of their own, often smaller congregations in outlying rural communities. I was not looking to minister in any official capacity: I was looking for a sizable suburban church with a lot of young people and activities, solid preaching, and a music ministry I could join. I expected that in such a big town there would be any number of churches that would welcome a seminarian as a musician and a Bible teacher. That turned out to be a terribly difficult thing to find, and over the next ten years, it didn't get any easier. Being single, a woman, and a seminarian turned out to be three strikes against me, and I found myself initially welcomed, then excluded, from one church after another.

The first church I joined was Highview Baptist, out past Buechel, which was also attended by SBTS president Dr. R. Albert Mohler, Jr., along with several other new faculty members (*new* being code at that time for *conservative*). The congregation was staunchly conservative, politically as well as theologically, and made up of a slightly older, solidly middle-class crowd. There weren't a lot of young people my age, but several of my seminary friends were also members, and that was enough for me. Right when I joined, however, the pastor and the music minister resigned in separate sex scandals that were prominent enough to be covered by the local media. They did not go quietly, either—they made tearful confessions from the pulpit at the end of service, pleas for forgiveness and prayer. I was too new to have a sense of how the congregation was affected emotionally or spiritually by these developments, but the immediate result was that Dr. Mohler filled in as preacher for some weeks, along with other guest preachers, until they found an interim pastor, and then a permanent one.

About six months later, I started to teach Sunday School to tenth and eleventh graders, with one of my male seminary friends. We opened the hour together and then broke off into adjoining rooms: I taught the girls; he taught the boys. We styled ourselves after Regis and Kathie Lee—warm and energetic and funny and well-dressed. We had a great time. But after about a year, Highview's youth minister resigned, and his replacement imposed new standards for teachers, limiting the influence of women in the church. Without warning, women were relegated to teaching only young children; any woman teaching high school students was removed. The church gave responsibility for my class to another man. No one reached out to encourage me, to help me find other ways of serving, or even to explain why I was suddenly not qualified to teach a class with which I'd been doing so well. I started looking for another church.

Dr. Mohler had a new assistant that year, who, with his family, took me to another Southern Baptist church, thirty minutes south of town, where I got involved in the music ministry right away. Sunday morning was led not by a choir or an orchestra but by a band, one with real talent. I sang with them, and even played some percussion. This church had also recently and abruptly lost their pastor, so Dr. Mohler's assistant filled in as interim preacher. His children were both in high school; they had heard about my teaching at Highview and asked me to teach their Sunday School. But again, I had a hard time finding a peer group. There were no other seminarians, and no other young women. It felt a little lonely there, though I had the worship band. I didn't officially switch my membership, though. I was waiting for them to hire a new pastor. After a few months, the top candidate visited and served as guest preacher one Sunday morning, followed by an immediate up-or-down vote by the congregation, in the room, on whether to call him as pastor. And I just hated his sermon. The congregation voted overwhelmingly to hire him, but I felt I could not go back.

At that point, I had several friends who were attending the local Reformed Baptist Church just outside the Gene Snyder. The Reformed church is small, and they are *not* Southern Baptist. They are *reformed* as in Calvin and Luther: ultra-conservative, socially and politically, beyond anything to be found in the SBC. Their children are almost exclusively homeschooled. Their daughters do not go to college. And their men do not go to seminary; prospective pastors are trained by other pastors in the field, because seminaries are not in the Bible. In the Bible, new ministers (like Timothy, for instance) were trained by senior ministers (like Paul). Reformed Baptists see no need for any ministry outside or alongside the church. That's how conservative they are—if it's not in the Bible, it shouldn't exist.

The Reformed Baptists are strict Sabbatarians—they refer to Sunday as "the Lord's Day," and they do no work that day. They partake of no worldly entertainment. The day is set aside for two long worship services, with family meals and quiet talk in between.

When I attended, I found their worship particularly sincere; they sang every verse of every hymn in four-part harmonies. They sang from the *Trinity Baptist Hymnal*, whose songs are meatier and more conservative theologically than the Southern Baptist hymns—most of them are like singing straight scripture. All the verses (six sometimes), with a sung *"Ah-men"* at the end. There was no flashy orchestra or rockin' band here, only a piano, but everyone would sing heartily. Congregational singing was an essential part of worship. I purchased one of their hymnals so I could learn the songs and use the uplifting texts in my private devotional time.

The Reformed Baptists are also notable for their discipline. At the entrance to the sanctuary there are signs that indicate that "Silence Must Be Kept" within its walls, and this is obeyed. When worshippers come in those doors, they refrain from chatter, find their seats quietly and sit in prayer or contemplation of Scripture as they wait for the service to start. Even little children will sit in the service and never fidget or make a sound. There is a nursery, but it is only for babies and toddlers—three and four-year-olds regularly attend morning worship, participating in the singing and sitting silently through the readings and preaching and prayers. If a child at the Reformed Baptist church ever gets even remotely out of line, one or the other parent leans down and whispers in his ear, and the behavior stops immediately.

Like many other Baptist churches, the RBC meets for three services a week: Sunday morning and evening (along with a single congregational Sunday School class), and a Wednesday night prayer service. Sunday morning worship always includes a reading of a full chapter from the Old Testament and a sermon from the New Testament. Evening service is the reverse—a chapter of reading from the New Testament and a sermon from the Old Testament. Their practice is to study the entire Bible together, straight through, never skipping passages or leaving anything out, even when a text is difficult or confusing. They don't randomly jump around and pick a topic that seems relevant like most churches do—on Mother's Day, there will not be a Mother's Day sermon; on Super Bowl Sunday, football will never be mentioned.

The preaching is so solid and good—really the best preaching I've ever heard in terms of expounding on the Biblical text, opening up a text and explaining it historically but also applying it to contemporary life. As noted, I was spoiled by the seminary chapel sermons and my teachers there, but I learned something every time I attended the Reformed church. I loved the singing, the preaching, the sincerity of spirit there. I really got hooked on it and I attended every Sunday for months.

I visited one Wednesday for prayer meeting, but I was so distressed by the experience, I couldn't go again. Everyone gathers in the sanctuary, silently again, and they sit bowed forward or kneel on the floor as prayers are offered. But only men can pray out loud. A concern is raised, and the call goes out—"Who will pray for this concern?"—but only men volunteer, and only men are asked to offer prayer. Women are merely present, silently agreeing with the prayers of the men.

In fact, women are not allowed to speak in any way in any service at the Reformed Baptist Church. Sunday School involves the pastor or another elder teaching from the Scripture, and then a sort of question-and-answer session where people can ask more about the text or the teaching—except for women. No woman can even ask a question, because the Apostle Paul says,

"Women should remain silent in the churches. They are not allowed to speak, but must be in submission, as the Law says. If they want to inquire about something, they should ask their own husbands at home; for it is disgraceful for a woman to speak in the church" (I Cor. 14:34-35).

The only service women are allowed to offer is caring for babies and toddlers in the nursery or playing the piano. After worship, the men and women walk to different sections of the sanctuary for conversation. The women start talking about breastfeeding and homeschooling while the men start talking about theology. The women are taught not to concern themselves with theology. That is the men's purview.

So where was I supposed to fit in? I had no husband or children. The choices I had made in my life, to be single and pursue higher education, were not open to these women. My choices weren't ones anyone in that community really approved of. It was uncomfortable for all of us. So, I often walked over to talk to the men. Except they wouldn't talk to me. Even my seminary friends—good friends, who had classes with me, who knew my spirit, who I thought respected me—when I tried to contribute to a theological conversation in that setting, literally talked right over my head and ignored me.

One Sunday in winter, two seminary friends were visiting the Reformed church—a young, attractive couple, very popular on campus. I was glad to see them there, and we talked in a small group after the service, as everyone picked up their coats by the door. When my friend put on his coat, I saw that his collar was flipped backward, and I fixed it. A few minutes later, he and his wife took me aside and reprimanded me for having fixed his collar. They said my action was sexual, inappropriate, that it was not my place to touch another woman's husband's lapel. I was completely taken aback. It hadn't been my intention to be flirty, and even if it could be read that way, I couldn't see how my action was so bad as to rate this sort of intervention. But their personalities were stronger than mine, and they were teamed up against me. I could say nothing in my own defense, only apologize and say it wouldn't happen again. I would be more careful not to touch men in any way.

I felt humiliated, because they had assumed the worst of me, and particularly because I had not found language to defend myself. I cried a little bit on the drive home. Looking back, I feel ashamed again, that I couldn't come up with a stronger response. But even now, I am hard pressed to think of what I could have said that would have worked against people who saw themselves as superior and single women as threatening. People are so rarely rude to me, and I am conditioned to be gentle. My instinct is still to walk away and cry.

By nature, I am a warm, Puerto Rican, touchy-feely, kiss-you-on-the-cheek sort of girl, but after this confrontation, I felt like I had to become hypervigilant about not touching men. I remember feeling simultaneous humiliation and resentment. I was as chaste as any preacher could wish an unmarried young woman to be. I had learned in college to wear more clothes than felt natural to me, not to sit on people's laps or touch their hair while we talked, that such behaviors would be read as flirtation, which was not my intention. I had resented it, having to accommodate a culture that felt uptight, restrictive. But I had not rebelled then, and I didn't now. Either I wasn't angry enough—and anger was not an emotion I often let myself feel—or I wasn't courageous enough to act on it. I let myself be silenced.

It was a different confrontation that led me to leave the Reformed Baptists. I got into Southern Seminary's PhD program in ethics, and I was excited. I had been strongly encouraged by many faculty members in the School of Theology; in fact, the seminary had worked hard to put together a program for me, because we'd lost several ethics professors in political turmoil. I had been working toward this for years and finally got my letter of acceptance. I was going straight from the MDiv into the PhD, without a break. On my way out after the next worship service, I stopped to talk to the pastor. I was eager to share my good news, expecting that he would be glad for me. Shaking his hand, I told him, "Pastor, I got into the PhD program!" And his face fell. He almost cringed.

Again, all I could do was walk away. I suddenly realized that my academic advancement might feel like a threat to people who don't think women should be college-educated—the idea of a woman with a PhD, who could actually *teach* college, must have been unnerving. Also, this degree would make me more educated than the pastor. But I hadn't considered that I might face real opposition, and so it didn't occur to me not to speak about it. I knew then for certain there was no place for me at the Reformed Church, even as a visitor.

When Southern Seminary opened its doors in Kentucky, Jim Crow laws there prohibited any college or institution from educating both whites and "members of the Negro race." But in fact there were several Black students who would sit in the hallway and listen to lectures. Some faculty also offered these men private tutorials in their offices. In a few years, the first Black seminarians graduated, without having ever been in a classroom. In 1999, the Clarence Jordan Center started a scholarship fund for Black students, in the names of these first African-American graduates, and I helped plan a big worship service to celebrate. Pastor Charlie Davis of Hunsinger Lane Baptist Church was one of the white pastors who helped participate and brought his choir. This was my first contact with Charlie and his church, and through the process of putting together this scholarship fund event, I found that two of my favorite faculty members were both attending Hunsinger Lane.

When I first visited, on a chilly autumn Sunday, Hunsinger Lane Baptist was a very small, one-room church with swirly, opaque-pastel glass windows and a single piano. It looked dinky compared to those with big orchestras and spacious foyers—but God's Spirit was there. The preaching was less intellectual than what I'd heard at the Reformed Church, with fewer references to Greek and Hebrew, for example, but just as passionate and thought-provoking. Also, the church was so small that they only had morning services, which I liked because it gave me more free time on the Lord's Day (the Reformed Baptists had sold me on calling it that). Ever since college, I had made a special practice of keeping the Sabbath—I never went shopping or out to eat on Sundays (unless others invited me, under which circumstances it wasn't gracious to refuse).

Several other seminary students were then visiting worship services at Hunsinger Lane, including my two friends from the PhD program. We were both concerned for the same thing—to find a church that would let us teach adult Bible classes, a goal that had eluded us both thus far.

I asked the pastor the third week I visited: could I serve at all as a teacher? His response was something along the lines of, "Sure—we have a woman who teaches adult Sunday School; she's married, and her husband is in the class, and helps lead it. But she does the teaching." But the fact that she was married, with her husband in attendance, did seem to imply that a single woman like me would have a tougher time finding such a position.

It was a regular occurrence during that season of my life to be asked by new acquaintances whether I was married. *Not married? Are you engaged? Seeing anyone?* It was more than a little awkward. I became adept at waving aside these questions with phrases like, "I'm focused on serving the Lord right now," or, "I'm very happy, thank you." Within the first few days after arriving in Louisville, I heard for the first time the old joke about women coming to school for their "MRS degrees." I didn't think it was funny, but I also didn't realize how true it was at SBTS, how strong and continuous the pressure was to marry. Certainly, the society of the powerful seemed to have no unmarried members.

The pastor made it clear to me at the same time that, while his church was at least nominally pro-woman, they were not necessarily pro-seminary. It seemed to me that the pastor, if not the congregation, had felt somewhat hurt by the recent turmoil and turnover at the Southern Baptist Seminary. Even under normal circumstances, seminarians are only around for about three years, he explained—they join sometime within their first year, they serve for two, maybe, and then they're gone. This pastor didn't find that sort of upheaval helpful for his church. He wasn't against the seminary per se, but he wasn't excited to have a bunch of seminarians looking to join his church.

Eventually, I did join this congregation. I had visited for several months, waiting to feel more accepted by the church—waiting, more specifically, for someone to offer me a Sunday School class. They let me sing solos without joining choir; in fact, I sang a lot, and started giving the pastor's oldest daughter voice lessons. But I never got to do any teaching.

That was the only sour spot at my new church—yet again, not being allowed to teach. And the thing is, in Baptist life, if you're not *teaching* Sunday School, you're supposed to be *in* Sunday School. And one of the things I absolutely hate about Sunday School is that, at least in the Baptist world, they separate you into groups according to your gender and marital status. Which put me in the "singles" group. I would be the oldest one there, and that didn't feel so good. Most of my friends were in the "Young

Marrieds" class. As a seminarian, I didn't feel the need to go to Sunday School. I skipped it altogether, arriving after the teaching hour just in time for worship.

The year after I joined, the church built a new, larger building on a nearby property, and we all helped, putting up drywall and wiring and paint. With new education spaces, new classes opened up, and there was one adult class I was hoping to teach, so I went to visit it one Sunday morning. It was a big class, about thirty people in their thirties and forties. Now, the basic Sunday School model is to read a Bible passage and have people comment on what they think it means. And over and over in that one class session, I heard comments like, "Well, you know, it doesn't really take a PhD to understand this text." "I'm just glad I can come to God without a PhD;" "I'm so glad we can read the Bible without a PhD."

These were continual insults towards graduate students, with several of us right there in the room. While I never made an issue of it, I don't think anyone in the church was unaware that I was a doctoral student, that several other seminary students and faculty (with PhDs) were also attending their church with a good will. But at Hunsinger Lane I encountered a palpable anti-intellectual bias that I found surprisingly painful. In ordinary society, people commonly say things like, "Well, it's not rocket science," or "It's not brain surgery," but I don't think these comments are meant to devalue the work of scientists or surgeons. At this church, a common mantra was, "Well, I don't have a PhD, but I think the text means …." From these constant little digs, I got the clear message that I was not welcome, as a thinker or as a teacher. Instead I was again seen as a threat. Looking back, I think class difference was key in why I couldn't fit in at this church—they were not ready to accept people with advanced degrees, and they seemed even less ready for those people to be women.

As I entered the PhD program, I was required to travel to Oxford, England each year for several months. Around the second time I returned from England, the director of the Seminary Choir also returned from a sabbatical overseas at Cambridge University. We had clashed in previous years, but suddenly we had a real connection. We had long talks about how different church and culture were in England, and the challenges of returning to seminary life. Like most of our faculty, he served a local church, as the music minister at Highland Baptist. The director suggested I come there and sing in his *other* choir. He said Highland was more inclusive of women, like the English churches are.

Highland Baptist was different from any church I'd been a part of at that point—it was moderate-to-liberal, which was uncomfortable for me. I was used to the talk about Jesus being along the lines of, "eternal God-man who lived a sinless life, died on a cross, was buried and physically rose from the grave to redeem a sinful humanity." Highland's Jesus-talk is more, "Jesus is the full expression of the mystery of God," which initially made me squirm a little. The worship at Highland is "higher," more formal, liturgical. The ministers wear robes; they chant the Doxology in every service; they read Scripture from the lectionary, and the sermon is based on the Gospel reading.

I started going to Highland Sunday mornings, and to choir practice on Wednesday evenings. I was not attending chapel much anymore—the authoritarian, patriarchal atmosphere was crushing. But on Sunday evenings, Highland Baptist hosted Vespers, the weekly worship service of Sojourn, an edgy, progressive church several of my seminary friends were starting.

Sojourn's congregation was made up of a few dozen young people from Louisville and Southern Indiana. It felt like an underground movement of Christian hipsters—microbrew coffee-drinking, art-appreciating, creative young people who wanted a church of their own. They wanted a church that felt more authentic than the stiff, boring, controlling ones they'd grown up in. They wanted to be able to wear blue jeans and show their tattoos; they wanted exuberant live music and energetic sermons, and Sojourn gave it to them. Les was the quiet, shepherd-y leader behind the scenes and Daniel was the fiery preacher, backed by talented young musicians who wrote their own worship songs.

Sojourn had a distinct aesthetic: they used the all-lower-case lettering that characterized millennium-era electronic communication; their space featured exposed brick, an urban coffee-shop vibe, and was centered in the Highlands, the artsiest Louisville neighborhood. And their ministry was centered around the notion of community—reaching in—and connectedness to the city of Louisville—reaching out. For their logo, Sojourn adopted Louisville's symbol of the fleur-de-lis.

Sojourn started out small, just a few families and couples, but within a few months, there were hundreds of us attending worship, and at least a hundred in community groups. No one was officially a member at that point, because the church had yet to establish a formal constitution with the Southern Baptist Convention. Within a year, though, Sojourn was constituted—and that process spelled the beginning of the end for me.

In the beginning, the experience was organic and dynamic; there was a real sense of possibility. Church could be anything we wanted it to be. We could fix all the problems we saw with traditional Southern Baptist churches. At first, Sojourn was conceived in terms of a lot of things we *didn't* want, like Sunday School with married and single people being separate. We wanted more connection among the church body, through groups formed based on the geography of neighborhoods. We didn't want hymnals; we didn't want pews. If you wanted to lie down in worship, you could—if you wanted to kneel, or sit, if you wanted to raise your hands, or dance, you had that freedom. No one was going to be watching you, or tell you what to wear, what to do when. There would be, at some points, an *invitation* to stand and sing, for example, but no one would think a thing of it if you sat. There was going to be real freedom in worship.

We planned to do away with the traditional litmus tests of the evangelical movement and the seminary—we were not going to judge people or exclude them based on their politics. There was not going to be a check-the-box ethics, where everyone had to have the same priorities and moral values. There was not going to be an attitude of, only if you have the same demographics as I do can you be my friend, or part of this group or ministry. We wanted to create an experience that would be comfortable for people who might not feel so welcome in other churches.

Someone found us a property, a little storefront on Bardstown Road, and turned it into a gallery. It was a raw space with exposed brick and a small bathroom, and we all worked together to make an office space in the back and an art gallery in the front. The opening exhibition was an amazing collection of pen-and-ink sketches from the Vatican, and the opening reception allowed us to practice hospitality to each other and our neighbors in the Highlands. In the early months, we worshipped in the gallery and had concerts and meetings there. We named it "Aslan's How," a reference from C.S. Lewis' *Prince Caspian* to a sort of lair, a hideout for the faithful.

Our ministers were fans of Lewis and G.K. Chesterton, readers of literature as well as theology. They brought an appreciation of art and nature to the community and shaped it accordingly. Because of their leadership, the idea was strong at Sojourn that God can be found in all art, nature, and beautiful things. Sometimes, we would have worship in the park. It was a humanist view which I found refreshing. And that this movement was being led by my peers, couples who were my own age, was part of the appeal. I didn't see them as authoritative in the way my earlier pastors had been. We could be a team.

There have been only three brief seasons in my life when I was popular. One was my first year of college. I had friends in the dorm, and the Baptist Campus Ministry: there were thousands of people on campus, so it was easy to have a hundred friends. When I was in Oxford, I was popular with students about ten years younger than myself. Perhaps because I was older and more confident, I was able for the first time to be a social leader, to initiate gatherings and pull together impromptu events, but I was only there a few months of the year for two years.

But I felt super-popular at Sojourn. At twenty-nine, I was almost the oldest person there. There were a lot of younger women in their early twenties who seemed to look up to me. The church had me teach a few classes, and Daniel even let me speak in worship once. I hung out with the worship team, we wrote songs together, and I learned to create harmonies and play percussion instruments. I had more social opportunities than I had since college; there wasn't a day my phone didn't ring. I felt connected and valued and happy.

Then Sojourn started to change, to be more like the churches I had already had to leave. The leadership at that point was essentially made up of three men: two pastors and a worship leader. They held several church-wide meetings to discuss our vision for the future of Sojourn. One of the main points of discussion was how, in traditional SBC churches, women couldn't serve as pastors or elders. And the leaders said that Sojourn would be more open. The senior pastor would be Daniel, of course—but women would definitely serve as deacons and elders. I felt so encouraged. Finally, a congregation where I could serve and use all my gifts! It even seemed that the role of pastor was going to a man specifically because it was Daniel's role, rather than that the pastorate being reserved solely for men on principle. But a year later, when it came down to officially framing the constitution, no women were asked to be deacons, and it was decided that no women would serve as elders.

Behind closed doors, it was also decided that divorced people could not serve at Sojourn, which had started at the home of a man who was now divorced and so no longer in leadership in the church. Certain other issues about sexuality also started coming up at church. The Highlands neighborhood in Louisville has a great many gay, lesbian, bisexual, and transgender people, and they had always been welcomed at Sojourn. But in the summer of 2002, Daniel preached a sermon series from Genesis on gender and sexuality, with the goal of clarifying what he called "gender confusion" in our local community and American society. He came out strongly against homosexuality, even though when Sojourn started, everyone was welcomed equally. Now, apparently, gay folk were welcome, *but* they should go through some therapies to be healed of their perversions. He also opposed singleness, and the inclusion of women in leadership positions. Women's proper sphere is the home, so they don't belong in a leadership position outside the home. It was hard not to take it personally, or imagine my friends thought I was not fulfilled as a woman because I was not a wife and mother.

Suddenly it seemed that all sexuality was a threat, best handled by getting everyone safely married and pregnant. That had surely been the culture at the seminary, and the other Louisville churches I'd been a part of. I had gotten the same comments from pastors, seminary faculty, and their wives. My own mother never urged me to get married or procreate—but there were plenty of strangers who didn't hesitate to exhort me on the subject. I did not sense God in any way calling me to marriage, and no one was interested in marrying me. I did not stay up nights pining for a mate or struggle with lustful thoughts. Yet I was told countless times that I was "pricing myself out of the marriage market by getting too much education"—by pursuing my own gifts and my own path I was closing doors to finding somebody who would love and accept me. Then the overall bias against higher education that I experienced in other churches began to show itself here as well, and I noticed other Sojourn members dropping out of higher education or deciding not to pursue university or graduate school at all.

I confronted Daniel after his first sermon, reminding him that many single folk were perfectly happy in their condition, and that Scripture supported such a lifestyle. He reassured me, *Of course, of course,* that wasn't his main point, it wouldn't be an issue. Nevertheless, he kept returning to these themes, week after week, all summer.

I left Sojourn quietly on my own in silent protest, which did not feel like enough. I was angry, not at individual people so much as at the bigoted views hidden under spiritual language, the harsh policies cloaked in religious profundity and Bible quotes. I withdrew into more private spirituality for several years, away from religion, from religious people and their expectations.

It would take me several more years to find my way to churches led by women, and only now have I fully entered into the lengthy and challenging process of seeking ordination. I try to tell myself that we see what we can see when we can see it, but I struggle with regret that I stayed in these restrictive communities for so long, when more open ones were right around the corner. I struggle with self-recrimination that I was not able to shift the culture in these Baptist churches of Louisville, my hometown for twenty-five years. I grieve the loss of the friendships I made in these congregations and pray for greater unity in the Body of Christ and the city I love.

Someday

STEVEN MICHAEL CARR

When David walked into Cafe 360 at 10:30 p.m. on a Monday night one January, I noticed him. I was sitting with my friend Joe, enjoying a hookah while we waited for our shifts to start at UPS. I leaned over to Joe and said, "That guy is cute," and took a long drag from the hose, smoke rolling out of my mouth.

Joe smiled and slow-blinked and maybe even bit his lip a little, as if he could not believe his luck. "Remember how I told you I went on that date with that guy a few weeks ago," he said, "and I never called him back? Well, that's him."

Much to Joe's chagrin, David saw us and trotted right over and said hello. The next thing I knew he had sat down with us and he and Joe started a dance that can only be described as *verbally sparring in Southern*, where both parties take shots at each other in pleasant yet passive-aggressive tones.

It's so nice to see you!

Yes, you must be so busy! I haven't heard a peep from you!

Well yes, you know how it is. You look well!

Joe promptly made his excuses and left.

David stayed.

I had only been out of the closet for a month, and he was the first man I felt affection toward that reciprocated.

The next Saturday I took him along to my monthly midnight viewing of *The Rocky Horror Picture Show* at Baxter Avenue Theater. The weekend after that, we went to church together for the first time at Highland Baptist Church, which David had found on a website called Gay Christian Network. I had been attending Sojourn Community Church, known to many as the "tattooed hipster church," until fairly recently when the pastor had, from the pulpit, said that gay people were only allowed to join if they acknowledged their lifestyle as sinful and promised to turn to celibacy. I was newly out of the closet and I was not about to head back in.

David had talked to a member of Highland Baptist who said that it was an open and affirming church. I was raised as a Southern Baptist and had never heard of such a thing. To me, being a Baptist meant that being gay was a sin, as was drinking, dancing, and women holding positions of power. I was skeptical that this Baptist church was going to welcome us.

And yet we showed up that Sunday and did not catch on fire when we walked into the sanctuary. The message was one of love. The music lifted my spirit like it used to before the church became a symbol of hate for me.

After the service, a man in his mid-twenties approached us and said that some young adults from church were having brunch at an apartment down the street and that they'd love it if we could join. He introduced himself as Ryan and then introduced his girlfriend, Jill. David and I looked at one another and agreed.

But as we left the church and began to walk the block and a half down the street to the brunch party, I leaned toward David. "Do they know we are gay? Is this okay? Is this a trap?"

He didn't know.

My anxiety rose as we stepped up to the door of the apartment.

David knocked. I held my breath.

The door opened and a man with a deep tan, immaculate haircut, and a Dolce and Gabbana belt buckle shouted *Heeeeyyy* in the San Francisco accent of our people and we knew that this was a safe space. He and the others gave us food, placed mimosas in our hands, and within minutes we were all fast friends.

David and I jumped right into church life. We joined ministry groups. We sat on committees. We even helped start an LGBTQ ministry at Highland called True Colors with our friend Maurice in an effort to let members of that community know that God loves them just the way they are. That small group started marching in the Kentuckiana Pride Parade with about eight people, and it grew until now over one hundred folks from our church walk in the parade each year.

How funny it is that church was what rejected me as a gay man, and yet it was also church that would come to affirm me as a gay man. We embedded ourselves in the ebb and flow of the church and it became our home.

There was only one thing about this home. It had never performed a same-sex wedding before. Not because it was morally opposed. It's just that nobody had ever asked.

———————

David is four years older than me, and once he hit his mid-twenties, his friends all started to get married. At first he went to these weddings alone. We had been dating for about a year and neither one of us knew the appropriate length of time before you bring your significant other to a wedding. At least that's what we told ourselves.

In reality, we did not want to cause a scene. Two men clearly together at a string of Catholic weddings would definitely catch the eyes of the other guests. People would talk. Some people might even have a problem, and that day shouldn't be about us. We did not want to be a bother.

So I stayed behind. But his friends knew we were in a relationship and always asked, "Where is this Steven I keep hearing about?" And after attending a few of these weddings that always prompted that same question, David asked me if I wanted to attend the next one with him.

"Wedding" for me up until that point meant a stodgy affair in which people recited the same scripture, said the same things, had an altar call, and then everyone drank punch. "Wedding" meant dull. Boring. I agreed to attend, but I let David know that I was doing this out of a sense of obligation and not because I intended to have any fun. David told me that I was wrong, that we would have a great time.

And he was correct! For starters, there was an open bar. And I got to meet David's friends from college. It wasn't awkward at all until it came time for slow dancing.

Every one of those college friends got up to slow dance with each other. Heads on shoulders and arms draped around necks. Men and women looking into each other's eyes, entranced. I remember thinking about asking David to slow dance with me, but not feeling comfortable enough to do so. We looked at one another, sipped our wine, and held hands under the table.

When it came time for the "How long have you been married?" dance to commence, we watched all of the married couples get up and sway back and forth. One year. Three years. Five years. People exited the floor as their time was up. They took their seats.

Ten years. Twenty years. Thirty-five. Fifty. Until one lone couple stood, wrinkled and with delight, their relationship aged like the bottles of Pappy Van Winkle we all wanted but could not afford.

David leaned into me and said, "I want that someday."

"Me, too," I said, and we both sighed and rested our faces in our hands as we looked on. "Maybe someday."

During the summer of 2011, from May to September, David and I attended eight weddings. Most of them happened in churches, none of which were open and affirming. It is an interesting feeling, celebrating people you love in a space that does not love you. The priest or pastor knows it and can tell by the way your clothes fit and the fearless way you wear pink. The wedding couple knows it and they chose the church anyway because it looks good in pictures.

And you know it. You can feel the weight of it as soon as you walk into the sanctuary.

But it isn't about you. It's never about you. You don't say anything. Affirming your relationship in a sanctuary isn't a thing. It isn't your special day so you don't make it about yourself. You tell yourself these things and then you stuff those feelings down and you move on to the reception and you drink your glass of wine and you boogie on the dance floor and everyone tells you you're one hell of a dancer and you thank them and you sit down during the slow songs. Because you don't want to be a bother. It was not any one person's fault. It was not intentional. It never is. But it's there. And you feel it.

Until one day when we decided that we did want to be a bother.

Maybe it was the wine or maybe we were finally tired of sitting on the sidelines, but at one of those summer weddings, David held his hand out to me as the notes of "At Last" by Etta James began to play and said, "We are going to dance."

I was not sure.

"This is going to be for our entire lives," he told me. "We need to get used to it. Let them stare."

And that settled it. I took his hand and we walked arm in arm to the dance floor, and we became one of the many couples rotating that slow circle. We clung to each other in front of everyone, hands on waists—and eventually, once the ceiling didn't collapse, heads on shoulders. I whispered the words into his ear. It felt right. It felt whole.

And then it went into Louis Armstrong's "What a Wonderful World" and they began the "How long have you been married?" dance. The moment ended. We walked to our seats.

The following January, David and I decided we should talk with Highland Baptist Church about getting married in the sanctuary. It started as a conversation in our pastor's office, the three of us sitting on couches and chairs around a coffee table. David and I had been together for three years, and we told Pastor Joe Phelps that we wanted to get married. We wanted to get married in our sanctuary. We wanted to get married in our home.

We knew that as a Baptist Church, there would be lots of bureaucracy to work through. Baptist churches are wholly autonomous, highly democratic, and self-governed. The blessing of being a Baptist is that you get to have a say in the operations and stances of the church. The curse of being a Baptist is that you have to have a say in the operations and stances of the church. It means business meetings and voting on bylaws and attending quarterly church conferences to make decisions about public stances on systemic racism, what's happening at our borders, or, in this instance, marriage equality.

We knew there would be a long hill to roll that ball down and we wanted to get it rolling.

Pastor Joe was happy to hear that we were talking about marriage. You could see it in his eyes when he smiled. And yet, he said, with all that was going on in the church around whether or not people from other denominations should be able to join without getting re-baptized, he asked us to wait. "Let's look at this in a year so that it will be more likely to go through," he said.

And so we waited. We showed up to meetings. We voted on bylaw changes. We marched in the pride parade again, wondering if it really was appropriate for us to do so when David and I couldn't walk down the aisle together. We talked to people at our church's booth at the Kentuckiana Pride Festival, feeling like it wasn't fair that we had to wait, but also recognizing that this was bigger than us, and maybe it was our cross to bear. That, like it or not, we were locked in a game of chess, with the spoils of victory being our basic human right to marry each other.

That summer we took a trip to Washington, D.C. and to Massachusetts to visit friends. We thought we might go ahead and get legally married while we were in Massachusetts. I talked with my mom about it. I told her that we might go ahead and get the legal stuff taken care of while we had the opportunity. She sighed and said that it would be hard for her to get a ticket last minute to fly to Massachusetts because she wanted to be there. But she understood our need to get things done.

I talked with my dad and he said, "Are you sure? Is this what you want to do?" I told him that I was sure. He said, "If you're sure, then I'm sure."

Ultimately, it didn't matter. When it came time to head north, David could not find his birth certificate and we did not end up having the documents necessary to get married.

I was annoyed about this for a day or two, but the trip to D.C. ended up being glorious. Our friend Jeremy took us around the capital, showed us museums, restaurants, and bars. He showed us the church he attended. And then, during a quiet moment at the reflecting pool by the Lincoln Memorial, David pulled me aside and held my hand.

The next thing I knew, he was getting down on one knee.

"What are you doing?" I said. "Get up! You're causing a scene!"

And then he pulled out a ring and everything stopped. Everything went silent. It was just the two of us, and Jeremy a few feet away with a camera that he had brought because this had been planned. This was not a spur-of-the-moment decision.

There were hundreds of people around. It was broad daylight in Washington D.C., and here David was making this grand gesture. We had never even held hands in public before—we felt it was too dangerous.

"Will you marry me?" David said. And he slipped the ring on my right hand instead of my left because he was so nervous. I was terrified that people would see us. That they would know. That someone would say something hateful.

I hurriedly replied *yes* and pulled David up from the ground. I blushed.

And then someone did say something.

A family of six, led by a woman probably in her early fifties, stopped. I expected them to be disgusted, like that time a man saw David holding my hand in a darkened movie theater in Kentucky and leaned in to tell us he had a Louisville Slugger waiting for us in the parking lot. Instead, the woman looked into my eyes, smiled, and said in a soft voice, "Congratulations, sweetie."

We returned home, and after the year of waiting we knocked on Pastor Joe's office door and arranged another meeting for the day before Christmas Eve. Behind a closed door, he and the deacon chair, Kathy, told us, again, "not yet." Highland Baptist Church had just ordained its first openly gay minister, our friend Maurice, and the church had just gotten through a campaign to transition to three worship services and two times for Bible study. Transition after transition was happening in the congregation, and the general message coming from the congregants was, "Can we please just stay still for a moment and catch our breath?" Joe and Kathy said they were sorry. Kathy even cried when she said it. They wanted to hug us and affirm us and reassure us that they wanted this to happen, but that we had to choose the right time. They kept asking if we were okay.

We were so used to trying not to be a bother. We said yes. We were fine.

All of this felt like a slap in the face after Pastor Joe delivered a sermon that morning called "Law of Love Trumps Love of Law."

We were not fine. We wondered how long we would have to wait. We wondered why our church got to identify as "open and affirming" when we were starting year two of not being able to conduct a wedding ceremony in the church.

I wrote Pastor Joe an email saying that I was, in fact, not okay. That we were about to start planning our wedding, and if we ended up having to get married somewhere else, we would not be returning. If we married under a different roof, every time I walked into that sanctuary I would think, "This is where I was supposed to get married. This is the aisle I was supposed to walk down." I told him that if we could not get married at the church we certainly would not ask him to conduct the ceremony. That every time we walked through those doors it would be a reminder of the injustice that was done to us.

"Tick tock," I told him.

That Christmas felt bitter. The day after Christmas Pastor Joe sent me a response, saying he felt that I was right, and that after reflecting more, he felt it was time to move forward with the request.

We knew change would not happen immediately. We knew the cogs needed to spin and the gears needed to catch each other in the teeth of our church machine. The validation of our feelings was enough to keep us going.

Several months later the associate pastor, Nina, and the upcoming deacon chair, a pleasant man named Bob, met with David and I for lunch at a local spot called Ditto's. They sat across from us and talked about how the proposal had been brought before the deacon body. That a congregational conversation was in the works around hosting ceremonies in the church. They even said that things might have to be taken to a vote because that's how Baptists do church business.

At that time I was ready for whatever needed to happen. "Let them vote," I said. "Put it to a vote now. Let's see what happens."

But we had to prime the pump first. Get a feel for where people stood on the issue. It felt odd to say about a progressive church that had already ordained gay deacons and a gay minister, but that's where we were.

They suggested that we might not want to be in the room when these discussions were had because we would get to see the naked truth of some congregants' beliefs regarding our marriage proposal. They said the church would be made aware that a couple had come forward, but we would not be identified in any way. Of course, all of our friends at church knew it was us. They supported us through all the waiting and were ready to start a riot on our behalf.

But I wanted to sit in, I told Nina. I wanted to see for myself. If there was an opposition, I wanted to look them in the eyes.

Nina's own eyes began to water. "It's their home," she said. "I'm sorry, but this is so sad to me. Highland is their home and they just want to get married there and it's not right." She began to cry. "I'm so sorry."

Two separate emotions struck me at once. Part of me felt understood and wanted to reach out to Nina and welcome her into my sadness around the issue. She named the feeling. Here we were, being strung along by our home, the place and people that said they loved us. That named our gifts and affirmed us in every other way but this one.

The second emotion was anger. Not only did I have to carry my own emotional load and support my fiancé with his own emotions around this topic, but now this woman who had been married for years, who had children older than me, whose marriage was as easy as signing a document in a courthouse, was offering up her emotional load as well. Her sadness was about me and directed at me and in the moment I wanted to upend the table like Jesus overturned the tables of the money lenders in the temple. I had no grace to give in that moment. We were both so tired of people telling us "sorry" or "it's not fair." We knew it wasn't fair. We knew people were sorry. But those words did not mean anything anymore. They were just words people said.

When push came to shove, the church did not end up voting on whether or not David and I could get married. Word traveled fast and everybody knew that it was us doing the asking. In the end, the deacon body decided it would be inhumane to vote on the issue. To do so would be to vote on our humanity. The church sign proclaimed "Love Wins" and before the church could even make an official announcement to its congregants, the news went viral—a Baptist church had decided to conduct same-sex ceremonies even though they would not be recognized by the government.

Many of the church members found out about the decision through Facebook and begrudged not hearing it from the source. Most of them felt angry that they did not get to vote: not at the expense of our humanity, but for the chance to affirm us. And so in what can only be described as the most Baptist thing I have ever heard, the church voted instead to affirm the deacon's decision not to vote.

Journalists swarmed, wanting to know the identities of the couple planning their wedding. We weren't trying to be famous. We just wanted to get married. Pastor Joe kept us abreast of all the interview offers, but we turned them down because we did not want a circus. I did not want to read the comments section about my own wedding. We did not want our words twisted by someone who could not understand the depth of what our story meant. David and I only agreed to an interview when a journalist who reached out identified himself as gay.

We sat down at O'Shea's on Baxter Avenue and within moments we knew that our story would be safe. He asked us about what it was like to be activists. We told him we weren't.

He asked us where we planned on traveling to complete the legal part of our union. I told him I hoped we wouldn't have to travel. That I had so much pride in my city and I thought that it might pull through.

The article appeared on the front page of the Sunday *Courier Journal*. The phone calls rolled in. My grandmother let me know that she saved five copies—one of them she even framed. When we sent out the invitations, my Catholic Grandma Carr told me that she would be at the wedding. She told me she had sat down with her priest, Father Burke, and asked him if it was proper in the eyes of her parish that she attend my wedding, and he told her he thought she should. "It is not the life I would have chosen for you, Little Steve," she said. "But I love you and I love David and I will be there to celebrate you."

More articles appeared, riffing off of that initial article, until our names appeared in news articles in the United Kingdom. To this day I don't understand how one wedding ceremony in Kentucky made waves in Europe. Maybe it's because they thought we didn't even wear shoes, and here we were marrying gay people.

On May 23, 2015, which also happened to be my mother's birthday, David and I stood in the Fireside Room of Highland Baptist Church, helping each other put on our suits. We didn't wait to see each other until we walked into the sanctuary. We did what we always did: we supported each other. I helped David tuck his bow tie into the collar of his oxford shirt. He lint-rolled my jacket. We were the only two people in the room. It was holy ground.

We played Paper Rock Scissors to see who would walk down the aisle first, and then we exchanged rings and vows in front of three hundred people, a standing room only crowd.

When you're gay and you've lived together for as long as we had prior to our ceremony, you don't think anything will change after, and perhaps it doesn't if you only go to a courthouse and sign some documents. But up in front of all those people, literally everyone we knew and loved from all over the country, something felt different. It was then I realized that the covenant of our marriage, the spiritual pact we were making, was not just between the two of us. It was also between us and that room of people. They also made a pact: to hold us and care for our relationship. Everyone in that room was bound together, witnessing an occurrence that had never happened before in that space. We were the first.

When our friend Ryan finished his reading of Richard Blanco's poem "Until We Could" at the pulpit, his McConaughey-like accent hovering over the words, "...or how, when I hold you, you are rain in my hands," there was not a dry eye in the house.

We danced our first dance to the song "Home" by Edward Sharpe and the Magnetic Zeros in the Great Hall of the Kentucky Center for African American Heritage. David and I performed light choreography. Everyone clapped in time to the music. When it was time for my mother and I to dance, we slowly circled the dance floor to Louis Armstrong's "What a Wonderful World." Words that used to remind me of a world I could never live in now described a place in which I belonged.

And when it came time for the "How long have you been married?" dance, we asked the DJ to ask instead, "How long have you been together?"

Couples flooded the dance floor and began to sway back and forth to the Righteous Brothers' "Unchained Melody." The DJ began to call out years. We left the floor immediately, but this time it felt different. At least ten gay couples were still dancing.

One year. Three years. Five. Several of our friends from college, the folks whose weddings we'd attended over the past few years, left the floor.

Ten years. Fifteen. The floor began to clear. Still there remained several gay couples, people who would have gotten married if they could, or who had recently gotten married in other states, but had been together for what seemed like eternity.

Sixteen. Eighteen. And then twenty years and only grandparents remained. And our friends Bob and Brent, who had been together since the early nineties. Bob and Brent, who invited us to their small marriage ceremony in Millennium Park in Chicago the year before.

It was in that moment, seeing them dance, their heads nestled in each other's necks, unchained hearts filled with years of pushing forward, of glasses of wine and little arguments and sticking together through come-what-may, that I finally understood the meaning of the word pride.

David and I sat at a table during that dance, watching them. He leaned into me.

"I want that someday," he said.

"Me, too," I said. And I smiled. "And we'll have that. Someday."

CONTRIBUTORS

Emma Aprile lives in Louisville, Kentucky, on one of the streets she grew up on, in Tyler Park. She holds an MFA in poetry from George Mason University, and works as a copyeditor of literary fiction, nonfiction, and poetry for independent publishers, including Sarabande Books. She is also a part-time bookseller at Louisville's independent Carmichael's Bookstore, and her poetry has appeared in *Shenandoah*, *Antiphon*, *The Louisville Review*, and most recently, *Appalachian Heritage*.

Richard Becker is a Louisville-based union organizer and writer, working on and writing about income inequality, labor unions, and economic justice. His roots in Louisville run deep, as his ancestors settled throughout the Germantown and Paristown neighborhoods in the early twentieth century. He can be reached at becrichard@gmail.com.

Svetlana Binshtok is an essayist and fiction writer living in Chicago. She has also done storytelling with The Second City, 80 Minutes Around the World, and the Fillet of Solo Festival. She was born in the Soviet Union, the Eastern Rust Belt, and grew up in Cleveland before living in Louisville.

Caleb Brooks is director of International Service Learning at the University of Louisville. He grew up at the edge of Louisville's Iroquois Park, and spent a lot of formative days staring up at the synapse-silhouettes of winter oaks. He messed around and passed his post-undergrad twenties living in places like Cambodia, Liberia, India, and Brazil, because curiosity. But riparian roots run deep, and he's happy to be back along this little crack in the Ohio's limestone shelf.

Dan Canon is a civil rights lawyer and law professor based in New Albany, Indiana. He has bylines in numerous regional and national publications, including *Salon* and *Slate*. His regular column about civil and criminal justice issues is published by the *Louisville Eccentric Observer*. He also produces a short documentary series about Midwesterners who are making the world a better place called *Midwesticism*. His first book, *Pleading Out*, is scheduled to be published by Basic Books in 2021.

Steven Michael Carr is the Director of Development for Mattingly Edge, a Louisville non-profit. He is an active member of the local storytelling scene, an ordained Baptist deacon, and lives in Old Louisville with his husband David.

Ashleé Clark is the author of the book *Louisville Diners* (History Press) and the digital director at Louisville Public Media. She was born and raised in Louisville (Shively, to be exact).

Kimberly Garts Crum enjoyed a social work career in Iowa before moving to Louisville, where she received her MFA in writing. Now, she is the sole proprietor of Shape & Flow Writing Instruction, a studio located in a re-purposed slaughterhouse in Louisville. There, she teaches memoir and personal essay to aspiring writers who want to tell true stories, for posterity or publication. Kim is the co-editor of an anthology, *The Boom Project: Voices of a Generation.* She is working on the final draft of a segmented memoir titled, *Slouching Toward Self-Actualization.*

Olga-Maria Cruz is a poet and essayist who lived in Louisville from 1995 to 2016, where she earned the MDiv and PhD at The Southern Baptist Theological Seminary and taught at Bellarmine University. Her poems have appeared in journals including *Poetry East, Limestone, The Chaffin Journal, Pen & Brush,* and *Bellevue Literary Review.* Her chapbook, *A Philosopher Speaks of Rivers,* was published by Finishing Line Press. She has received poetry and creative nonfiction grants from the Kentucky Arts Council and Kentucky Foundation for Women.

Kathleen Driskell is the author of the poetry collections *Blue Etiquette: Poems,* a finalist for the Weatherford Award; *Next Door to the Dead,* a Kentucky Voices selection by the University Press of Kentucky and winner of the 2018 Judy Gaines Young Book Award; *Seed Across Snow,* a Poetry Foundation national bestseller; *Laughing Sickness* and *Peck and Pock: A Graphic Poem.* A professor of creative writing, she currently serves as Chair at Spalding's School of Creative and Professional writing and as Chair of the Board of Directors of the Association of Writers and Writing Programs.

Asha L. French is a writer from Louisville, KY. Her work has been published in *Pluck!, Ebony Magazine,* and *The New York Times.* She is a member of the Affrilachian Poets.

Ben Gierhart is a writer, playwright, and theater artist based out of Louisville, Kentucky. His play *Another Man's Treasure* won the Southeastern Theatre Conference's Getchell New Play Award in 2016. As a freelance journalist, he has written for Louisville Public Media, *Louisville Magazine*, *Queer Kentucky*, and other publications.

Martha Greenwald is the curator of Gathering: A Literary & Music Salon, based in Louisville, KY. Her poetry collection, *Other Prohibited Items*, won the Mississippi Review Prize. Her work has appeared in such journals as *Slate*, *Poetry*, and *The Threepenny Review*.

Timothy Noel Harris is a musician and writer living in New York City. He is the author of *Quizzical Venice* and *Iconoclysms: Shattered in Venice, Rome and Barcelona* (Torcello Editions). He played bass in the Babylon Dance Band and appears on many recordings by Antietam, Tara Key, and other artists. With Tara Key, Chip Nold, and others, he is writing *Babylon Revisited: The History of a Louisville Punk Rock Band*.

Dave Harrity's writing has appeared in *Verse Daily, Copper Nickel, Palimpsest, Memorious, The Los Angeles Review, Softblow*, and elsewhere. His most recent book is *Our Father in the Year of the Wolf* (Word Farm, 2016). He is a recipient of an Emerging Artist Award and an Al Smith Fellowship from the Kentucky Arts Council.

Idris Goodwin is a playwright and break-beat poet. His plays include *And In This Corner Cassius Clay, How We Got On, Hype Man*, and *This is Modern Art*. His poetry books include *Can I Kick It?* (Haymarket) and *These Are The Breaks* (Write Bloody). Goodwin serves on both the advisory boards of Theatre for Young Audiences USA and Children's Theatre Foundation Association. Idris is the director of The Colorado Springs Fine Arts Center at Colorado College.

Michael L. Jones is a freelance journalist and author based in Louisville, Kentucky. His book *Louisville Jug Music: From Earl McDonald to the National Jubilee* (History Press) received the 2015 Samuel Thomas Book Award for best local history from the Louisville Historical League.

Erin Keane lives under the flight path and around the corner from a secret cemetery in Louisville. The author of three collections of poetry, she teaches in the Spalding University School of Creative and Professional Writing and serves as Editor in Chief at *Salon*.

David James Keaton divided his Louisville days teaching at Elizabethtown Community and Technical College and playing trivia and vintage pinball at Zanzabar in Germantown. He followed Amy J. Lueck out West, where he writes fiction and teaches at Santa Clara University. They have a new daughter named Hazel.

Tara Key is a musician, visual artist, and writer living in New York City. She played guitar in the Babylon Dance Band. Key is a member of the band Antietam, with Timothy Noel Harris. Their latest record in a four-decade career is *Intimations of Immortality* (Motorific Sounds). Her visual art has been part of solo and group shows in New York, Louisville, and Chicago. She is at work on a book, *Friends Call, Strangers Cordially Invited*, about Gilded Age Louisville vice and the role of her ancestor Fannie Uhl Evans, a madam. With Timothy Noel Harris, Chip Nold, and others, she is writing *Babylon Revisited: The History of a Louisville Punk Rock Band*.

Susan E. Lindsey is coauthor and editor of *Speed Family Heritage Recipes*, a collection of original recipes from the family who built Farmington plantation in Louisville, Kentucky. Her latest book, *Liberty Brought Us Here: The True Story of American Slaves Who Migrated to Liberia*, is being published by University Press of Kentucky in mid-2020.

Amy J. Lueck attended graduate school at the University of Louisville, where she spent most of her time either hosting or playing pub trivia up and down Bardstown Road. She now lives in Santa Clara, California, where she researches and teaches writing as Assistant Professor at Santa Clara University.

Nancy McCabe's sixth book, *Can this Marriage be Saved: A Memoir in Essays,* is due out from the University of Missouri Press in fall 2020. Her poetry, creative nonfiction, and fiction have appeared in many journals and anthologies, including *Fourth Genre, Massachusetts Review, Newsweek, Los Angeles Review of Books, Michigan Quarterly Review, Prairie Schooner, Gulf Coast*, and *Every Father's Daughter: Women Writers Remember their Fathers.* Her previous books include the novel *Following Disasters* and the nonfiction book *From Little Houses to Little Women: Revisiting a Literary Child-*

hood. Her work has received a Pushcart Prize and seven times made notable lists in Best American anthologies. She directs the writing program at the University of Pittsburgh at Bradford and teaches for the Spalding University School of Creative and Professional Writing.

Dana McMahan, a fifteen-year Louisvillian, has covered the city's culinary and spirits scene for more than ten years for local and national outlets. She lives in the historic (and underdog) neighborhood Old Louisville with her husband and two dogs, where they share their Victorian with a parade of travelers in attic and carriage house Airbnbs.

Norman "Buzz" Minnick came of age in the 1980s punk scene of Louisville, Kentucky, and is the frontman for the influential hardcore band, Bush League. His previous collections of poetry are *To Taste the Water* (winner of the First Series Award from Mid-List Press) and *Folly* (Wind Publications). Minnick is the editor of *Between Water and Song: New Poets for the Twenty-First Century* (White Pine Press) as well as Jim Watt's landmark study of William Blake, *Work Toward Knowing: Beginning with Blake* (Kinchafoonee Creek Press). His chapbook of poems entitled *Advice for a Young Poet* (WordTech Communications) was published in 2020.

Derek Mong is the Byron K. Trippet Assistant Professor of English at Wabash College, located just 161 miles northwest of Louisville. He is the author of three books of poetry—*Other Romes* (2011), *The Identity Thief* (2018), and *The Ego and the Empiricist* (2017)—and one collaborative translation, *The Joyous Science: Selected Poems of Maxim Amelin* (with his wife, Anne O. Fisher, 2018). He grew up in Cleveland, lived in Michigan, and served as the Axton Fellow in Poetry at the University of Louisville from 2008-2010. He blogs at the Kenyon Review Online and can be reached at derekmong.com.

Ellen Birkett Morris is the author of the forthcoming short story collection *Lost Girls*. Her short stories and essays can be read in *Antioch Review*, *Shenandoah*, *The Butter*, on National Public Radio, and elsewhere.

Beth Newberry is an essayist and editor, and has moved back and forth from Kentucky to other places near and far, most recently living in southwest France for a few years, but always seems to find her way back home. Her work has appeared in *Sojourners*, *Salon*, *Louisville Magazine*, *The Louisville*

Review, Appalachian Heritage and *Still: The Journal*. Her essays have been twice named notable essays in *The Best American Essays* of 2011 and 2016.

Gwen Niekamp is originally from the Louisville Highlands and now lives in St. Louis, where she teaches English at Maryville University and creative writing at Washington University. From the latter, she holds both an MFA and a senior teaching fellowship in nonfiction writing. Her work is forthcoming from *Boulevard Magazine*. She is working on her first book, a memoir.

Chip Nold, under the byline James Nold Jr., has spent a thirty-year career as a freelance writer, editor, and researcher, with credits ranging from the *Village Voice* to the Museum of the American Revolution. He co-wrote two editions of *The Insider's Guide to Louisville and Southern Indiana*. In an earlier life, he was the lead singer for the Babylon Dance Band and the Bulls. With Timothy Noel Harris, Tara Key, and others, he is writing *Babylon Revisited: The History of a Louisville Punk Rock Band*.

Joy Priest is the author of *Horsepower* (Pitt Poetry Series, 2020), winner of the Donald Hall Prize for Poetry from AWP. Her work has appeared or is forthcoming in ESPN, *Gulf Coast, Mississippi Review, The Rumpus, Virginia Quarterly Review*, and *Best New Poets 2014, 2016*, and *2019*, among others. Priest is the winner of the 2019 Gearhart Poetry Prize from *The Southeast Review*, and the 2016 College Writers' Award from the Zora Neale Hurston/Richard Wright Foundation. She was the 2018 Gregory Pardlo Scholar at The Frost Place, the 2019 Nikki Giovanni Scholar at the Appalachian Writers' Workshop, and is the recipient of fellowships and support from the Bread Loaf Writers' Conference and the Fine Arts Work Center in Provincetown.

Brett Eugene Ralph is the author of *Black Sabbatical* (Sarabande 2009). He owns and operates Surface Noise, a record store/bookstore/art gallery/performance space in Louisville.

Almah LaVon Rice's work has appeared in *Tender, a literary anthology and book of spells: evidence; Black to the Future: A Collection of Black Speculative Writing; Queer Magic: Power Beyond Boundaries*; and other anthologies. Winner of the National Ethnic Media Award, she is at work on a speculative memoir about growing up in Louisville. She lives in Pittsburgh with her wife and all the books.

Aaron Rosenblum is a sound artist, curator, and librarian based in Louisville, Kentucky. His current project, Kentuckiana Sounds, is a community sound map of the Louisville metropolitan area and a podcast distributed by Louisville Public Media. He received a BA in experimental music from Hampshire College (2003) and a Masters of Library and Information Science from McGill University (2010). He lives with his wife and collaborator Andrea-Jane Cornell and their dog Lorraine on the western edge of the Schnitzelburg neighborhood.

Fred Schloemer, Ed.D, is a retired psychotherapist, former professor, and author. His book *Parenting Adult Children* won the 2012 Nautilus Book Award for books that promote positive social change. In 2015, LEO Magazine named his book *Behind the Footlights* one of the year's "must-read books by Kentucky authors."

David Serchuk is a writer, storyteller, and educator living in Louisville.

Ashlie D. Stevens is a food and culture writer whose work has appeared in and on *The Atlantic*, *National Geographic*, All Things Considered, Marketplace, and *Vice*. She is currently a staff writer at *Salon*.

Andrew Villegas is an editor at Colorado Public Radio in Denver. His journalism work has appeared in newspapers and radio stations all over the country, including *The Washington Post* and NPR. He holds bachelor's degrees in English and journalism from the University of Colorado in Boulder and his poetry has appeared in *Glass: A Journal of Poetry* and *The Acentos Review*.

Patrick Wensink is the bestselling author of six books. His most recent novel, *Fake Fruit Factory*, was named one of the best books of the year by NPR. He has published two picture books for children, *Go Go Gorillas* and *Gorillas Go Bananas*. His nonfiction is featured in the *New York Times*, *Esquire*, the *Oxford American,* and other outlets. He lives in Louisville, Kentucky, with his wife and son, and still listens to Wilson Pickett.

Brenda Yates is a prize-winning author of *Bodily Knowledge* (Tebot Bach). Her reviews, interviews and poems can be found in *Chaparral*; *The Tishman Review*; KPFK Radio 90.7 (Why Poetry); *The American Journal of Poetry*; *Mississippi Review*; *City of the Big Shoulders: An Anthology of Chicago*

Poetry (University of Iowa Press); *Angle of Reflection* (Arctos Press); *Manifest West* (Western Press Books); *The Southern Poetry Anthology, Volume VI: Tennessee* (Texas Review Press); *Fire and Rain: Ecopoetry of California* (Scarlet Tanager Books); *Unmasked: Women Write about Sex and Intimacy after Fifty* (Weeping Willow Books); and *Local News: Poetry About Small Towns* (MWPH Books) as well as journals based in Australia, China, England, India, Ireland, Israel, Portugal, and the Netherlands.

ACKNOWLEDGEMENTS

A version of "Nobody's Home" by Ellen Birkett Morris first appeared in *The Common's* Dispatches column.

"Falls of the Ohio" by Brenda Yates originally appeared in *DASH Literary Journal*.

"Too Bad the Whole World Swings Metal" by Derek Mong originally appeared in *Cimarron Review*.

"*The Wiz* Live from the Brown Theatre, Louisville, KY, December 2018" from *Can I Kick It?* by Idris Goodwin, © 2019 Haymarket Books. Reprinted by permission from the author.

"Tornado Warning/JoAnn Fabric & Craft" by Martha Greenwald originally appeared in *The Louisville Review*.

"Tachean Ho-Tep: Mummy at the Louisville Science Center" from *Next Door to the Dead* by Kathleen Driskell, © 2015. Reprinted by permission from University Press of Kentucky.

"Taking My Toddler to Wilson Pickett's Grave" by Patrick Wensink originally appeared in *The Weeklings*.

An earlier version of "Muhammad Ali's Hometown Heartbreak: I Went Looking for Ali's Louisville and It Wasn't There" by Dana McMahan originally appeared in *Salon*.

"A Peculiar Composition" originally appeared in the *Oxford American* Kentucky Music issue.

In "The Sanctified Present: Louisville Punk, 1978-1982," some of Tara Key's passages contain excerpts of her oral history for LUMA (Louisville Underground Music Archive). Portions of Chip Nold's passages contain excerpts from: James Nold Jr., "When Punk Rocked Louisville." *Louisville Magazine*: July 2007.

"Punk Rock" by Brett Eugene Ralph originally appeared in *Conduit #1*.

"Horsepower," "Derby" "Abecedarian for Alzheimer's," "God of the Motorcade," and "Drift" from *Horsepower* by Joy Priest, © 2020. Reprinted by permission from University of Pittsburgh Press.

"Air Devil's Inn on a Saturday Night" by Beth Newberry was first published in *MOTIF: Writing By Ear*, edited by Marianne Worthington (Motes Books, 2010). Reprinted by permission from the author.

An earlier version of "Where Have All the Rolled Oysters Gone?" originally appeared in NPR's *The Salt*.

"Et in Arcadia Ego" by Dave Harrity originally appeared in *Ninth Letter*.

"God and Tennis" from *Folly* by Norman "Buzz" Minnick © 2013 by Wind Publications. Reprinted by permission of the author.